CONTENTS

MARVEL 75TH ANNIVERSARY CELEBRATION

PAGE 20
THE BIRTH OF MARVEL

PAGE 58
YOUNG GUNS

PAGE 52
EVENT HORIZON

FROM THE EDITOR IN CHIEF

veryone remembers their first Marvel Comic. Mine was *Amazing Spider-Man #131*, which I bought off the rack at the five and dime on Clement Street in San Francisco when I was five. On the cover, Spidey crashes the wedding of his beloved Aunt May with a well-placed web-shot that prevents her from exchanging vows with the nefarious Dr. Octopus. I had no idea who any of the players on the cover were, but I simply had to know what was going on, why and how it all turned out. So I convinced my mom to shell out 20 cents, got my first taste of the Marvel Universe and whetted the appetite of a lifetime.

If you're holding this magazine, you probably have a similar story to tell. This magazine is a testament to 75 years' worth of stories that were someone's first dive into a modern mythology that's been handed down for generations. Stories that span — and blend — every type of genre and that reflect the world outside the window for three-quarters of a century.

It's my privilege to invite you to join the celebration of this landmark moment in Marvel's history. The *Marvel 75th Anniversary Magazine* offers an array of features on the birth of Marvel, Marvel toys, the biggest crossover events of the 1990s and 2000s, the 2014 Young Guns, digital comics, Marvel Studios, and the Top 75 Marvel comics of all time, along with interviews with Stan Lee and comic luminary Walter Simonson. It's a testament to the hard work and limitless imagination of the talented creators contained within and a reminder of Marvel's ever-expanding hold on the imagination of a global audience. At a time when someone's first taste of the Marvel Universe comes in so many forms — comics, both print and digital, movies, TV, animation, video games, and prose novels — what better time to reflect on how we got here and where it all began?

Axel Alonso
Editor in Chief

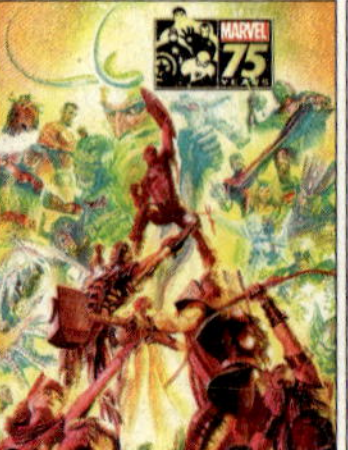

AN ASSEMBLY OF COVERS:
Greg Land's final art and Alex Ross's variants featuring the Fantastic Four, Avengers and X-Men.

MARVEL

Head Writer/Coordinator John Rhett Thomas
Feature Writers Robert Greenberger, Jess Harrold, Michael Kronenberg, Nathan Kronenberg, Dugan Trodglen & Tim Stevens
Design Evan Gubernick
Senior Editor, Special Projects Jeff Youngquist
Assistant Editor Sarah Brunstad
Associate Managing Editor Alex Starbuck
Editors, Special Projects Mark D. Beazley & Jennifer Grünwald
Editor in Chief Axel Alonso

Alan Fine *Office of the President, Marvel Worldwide, Inc. and EVP & CMO Marvel Characters B.V.*
Dan Buckley *President — TV, Publishing & Brand Management*
David Bogart *SVP of Operations and Procurement, Publishing*
Tom Brevoort *SVP of Publishing*
C.B. Cebulski *SVP of Creator & Content Development*
David Gabriel *SVP Print, Sales & Marketing*
Jim O'Keefe *VP of Operations & Logistics*
Dan Carr *Executive Director of Publishing Technology*
Susan Crespi *Editorial Operations Manager*
Alex Morales *Publishing Operations Manager*
Stan Lee *Chairman Emeritus*

MARVEL CUSTOM SOLUTIONS AND ADVERTISING

Jonathan Rheingold *VP, Custom Solutions & Ad Sales*
Niza Disla *VP, Partnerships Group*
Mitch Dane *Director of Custom Publishing*
Miriam Zafrani *Partnerships Manager*
Joshua Burrell *Project Manager, Promotions*
William Rosemann *Creative Director, Marvel Custom Solutions*
Mark Basso *Custom Solutions Coordinator*

For information regarding Marvel Custom Solutions and advertising, please contact Jonathan Rheingold at 646-742-6892 or jrheingold@marvel.com.

MARVEL LICENSING

Paul Gitter *SVP, Consumer Products North America*
Brian Siegel *Director of Franchise, MARVEL*
Susan Fields *VP, Product Merchandising, Softlines*
Rochelle Dick *Director of Merchandising, Softlines*
Isabelle Lahoud *VP of Licensing*
Michael Jerchower *Director of Licensing, Consumables*
Danny Kim *Director of Licensing, Softlines*
Meredith Norrie *Director of Licensing, Hardlines*
Joann McLaughlin *SVP of Product Development, Hardlines*
Jesse Falcon *Director of Product Development, Hardlines*
Mark Rhodes *VP, Marvel Retail Department*

For Marvel subscription inquiries, please call 800-217-9158.

SPECIAL THANKS TO BRIAN OVERTON, JOE HOCHSTEIN, JIM NAUSEDAS, DAVE ALTHOFF, TIM DILLON, WILL PILGRIM, ERIKA DENTON, & GREG BALDWIN

MARVEL 75TH ANNIVERSARY MAGAZINE. First printing 2014. ISBN# 978-0-7851-9333-3. Published by MARVEL WORLDWIDE, INC., a subsidiary of MARVEL ENTERTAINMENT, LLC. OFFICE OF PUBLICATION: 135 West 50th Street, New York, NY 10020. **Manufactured between 7/25/2014 and 8/19/2014 by R.R. DONNELLEY, INC., GLASGOW, KY, USA.**

10 9 8 7 6 5 4 3 2 1

HAPPY 75TH ANNIVERSARY, MARVEL

As a partner for the educational comic *Avengers: Saving the Day*, Visa Inc. congratulates Marvel on its historic 75th Anniversary. Thanks for helping Visa champion the important cause of improving financial literacy in youth around the world and bringing a unique approach to financial education.

CHECK IT OUT ONLINE
practicalmoneyskills.com/avengers

Avengers: Saving the Day is a free comic book that introduces children to basic financial concepts like saving and budgeting through the iconic Avengers. The heroes team up to defeat Mole Man and his evil army, all while learning important financial skills.

Practical Money Skills for Life™

CONGRATULATIONS
MAR
Thanks for 75 years of fantastic characters and
amazing storytelling that have inspired audiences around the world!
LEGO and the Minifigure figurine are trademarks or copyrights of the LEGO Group of Companies. ©2013 The LEGO Group. Characters featured in particular decorations are not commercial products and might not be available for purchase.

VEL!
POLY
LEGO
MARVEL
SUPER HEROES

THE HEROES OF FDNY

SALUTE THE HEROES OF MARVEL!

JOIN OUR TEAM!
JOIN FDNY

www.fdnyfoundation.org

GREATEST MARVEL COMICS OF ALL TIME

Earlier this year on Marvel.com and through our social-media channels, we put out the call asking you to help us select the 75 greatest comics in the history of the House of Ideas, and you came through—big time. With thousands of responses, narrowing down 75 years of the greatest characters and most talented creators did not prove an easy task—but with your assistance, we believe we came up with a representation uniquely Marvel. Enjoy 75 Fantastic, Amazing, Incredible, Uncanny gems from more than seven decades—as chosen by you!

75 The Death of Spider-Man

Ultimate Spider-Man #156-160

The Ultimate line has never flinched in the face of big changes, and none have been bigger than the death of that universe's Peter Parker in this emotion-filled event.

Collected in *Ultimate Comics Spider-Man Vol. 4: The Death of Spider-Man TPB*

74 Nextwave: Agents of H.A.T.E.

Nextwave: Agents of H.A.T.E. #1-12

HATE (Highest Anti-Terrorism Effort) was a group composed of the also-ran likes of Monica Rambeau, Machine Man and Tabitha "Boom Boom" Smith, in a wicked satire that featured Warren Ellis and Stuart Immonen doing whatever the heck they wanted with a super hero book.

Collected in *Nextwave: Agents of H.A.T.E. Ultimate Collection TPB*

73 New Mutants #98

Rob Liefeld and Fabian Nicieza continued to sow the seeds of X-Force with the introduction of Domino and—even bigger—Wade Wilson, aka Deadpool!

Collected in *X-Force Omnibus Vol. 1*

72 Marvel Two-In-One Annual #7

What's better than the Thing putting on a pair of boxing gloves and duking it out in a bout with the cosmic entity called the Champion? How about Colossus, Thor, Hulk, Sasquatch and other Marvel heroes joining him? This one's all about classic Marvel fun, courtesy of Tom DeFalco and Ron Wilson.

Collected in *Essential Marvel Two-in-One Vol. 4*

71 Fantastic Four #262

A decision to rescue Galactus from death ushers in "The Trial of Reed Richards," as the universe seeks to penalize Mr. Fantastic for condemning other planets to die. A complex tale by John Byrne that stands at the pinnacle of his epic run.

Collected in *Fantastic Four by John Byrne Omnibus Vol. 2*

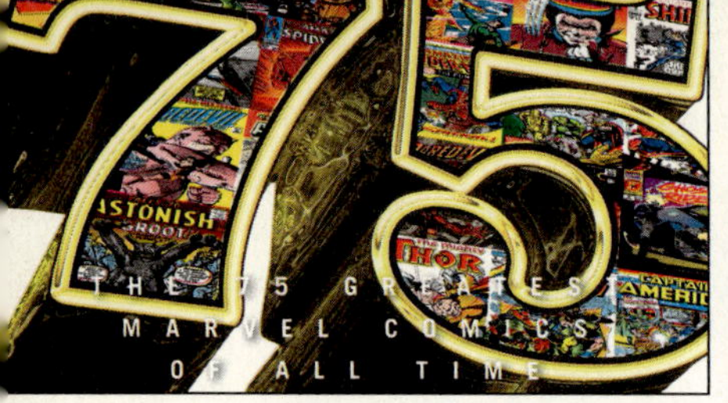

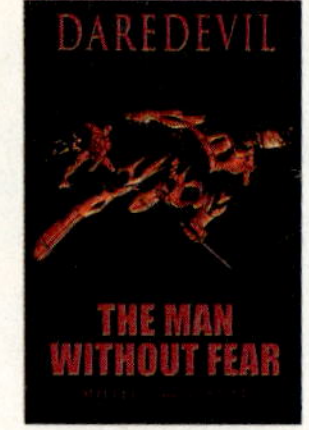

70 Daredevil: The Man Without Fear #1-5

Frank Miller returned to Marvel in 1993 to write this prestige limited series recounting Daredevil's origin, drawn by John Romita Jr. in one of the classic works of his career.

Collected in *Daredevil: The Man Without Fear TPB*

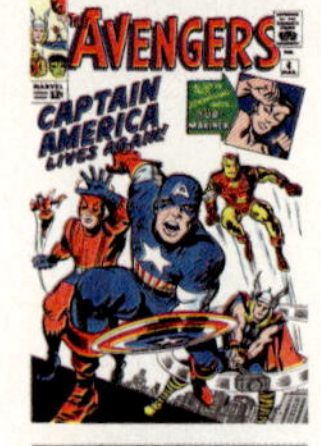

69 Avengers (1963) #4

The return of the Super-Soldier Steve Rogers, found on ice by the Avengers decades after his seeming death in the waning days of World War II. Can this man out of time be Captain America once more?

Collected in *Marvel Masterworks: The Avengers Vol. 1*

68 Amazing Spider-Man Annual #21

Wedding bells rang in 1987 for the event of the year: the union of Peter Parker and Mary Jane Watson! And they lived happily...ever... never mind.

Collected in *Marvel Weddings TPB*

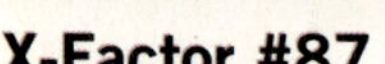

67 X-Factor #87

In one of the most novel stories of his legendary career, writer Peter David examines the X-Factor team through psychologist Doc Samson's eyes—with inspired visuals provided by new series artist Joe Quesada.

Collected in *X-Men: Fatal Attractions HC*

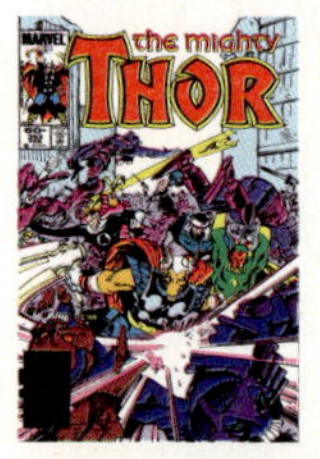

66 Thor #362

His fiercest foe...his staunchest ally? In the second of two standout issues from Simonson's run to make this list, Thor received unexpected aid from Skurge the Executioner, who held back the very forces of Hel itself so an Asgardian army could escape Hela's cold grasp. Never was a tale of heroic sacrifice more surprising—or more glorious!

Collected in *Thor by Walter Simonson Vol. 3 TPB*

65 The Clone Saga

In a mega-run that included just about every darned Spider-Man comic from 1994-1996, the Clone Saga was a love-it or leave-it proposition for Spidey fans. Its enduring appeal shows that a lot of folks loved it—including clone counterparts Ben Reilly and Kaine.

Collected in *Spider-Man: The Complete Clone Saga Epic Books 1-5 TPB* and *Spider-Man: The Complete Ben Reilly Epic Books 1-6 TPB*

64 Welcome Back, Frank

Punisher (2000) #1-12

The edgy Marvel Knights imprint gave Garth Ennis and Steve Dillon the freedom to do what they do best. The pair delivered a new Punisher for a new era—replete with over-the-top action and violence, and set in a generally self-contained universe that allowed Frank Castle the flexibility to do what he does best.

Collected in *Punisher: Welcome Back, Frank Premiere HC*

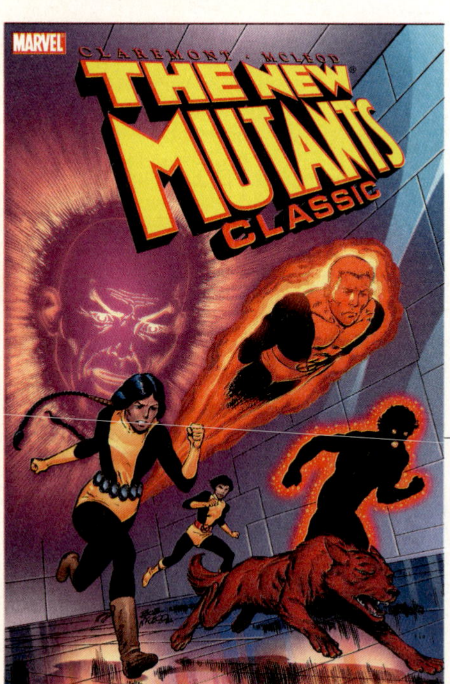

63 New Mutants by Chris Claremont

Marvel Graphic Novel #4; New Mutants #1-54, Annual #1-3

In the wake of the X-Men's runaway success, mutant maestro Claremont matriculated a fresh class of students at Xavier's School for Gifted Youngsters. The long-running '80s drama starring Sunspot, Magik, Mirage, Moonstar, Cannonball, Wolfsbane and their friends made for gripping reading.

Collected in *New Mutants Classic Vols. 1-7 TPB*

62 Marvel Comics #1

It all started here: the Timely first appearances of the Human Torch and the Sub-Mariner in creatively edgy stories that still have bite 75 years later.

Collected in *Marvel Masterworks: Golden Age Marvel Comics Vol. 1*

61 Silver Surfer: Parable

Silver Surfer (1988) #1-2

Stan Lee. Moebius. Silver Surfer. 'Nuff said.

Collected in *Silver Surfer: Parable Premiere HC*

60 Marvel Zombies

Marvel Zombies #1-5

The Walking Dead's Robert Kirkman was just the man to take a tongue-in-cheek coinage for Marvel fandom and turn it into a justifiable phenomenon. With parody covers by Arthur Suydam, phantasmagoric art by Sean Phillips and rending and consuming of human flesh by your favorite Marvel heroes, *Marvel Zombies* was the comic you never knew you wanted until it bit you in your wallet.

Collected in *Marvel Zombies: The Complete Collection Vol. 1 TPB*

59 Armor Wars

Iron Man #225-231

Tony Stark is the world's greatest weapons developer, but what happens when his deadliest technology winds up in the hands of a cabal of super villains? Armor Wars is what happens! A latter-day classic from the team of David Michelinie and Bob Layton!

Collected in *Iron Man: Armor Wars TPB*

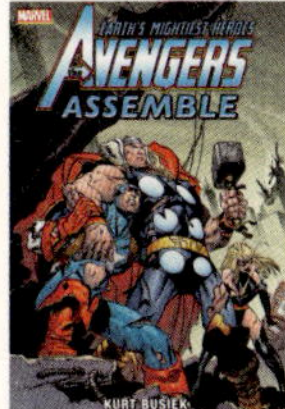

58 The Kang Dynasty

Avengers (1998) #41-55

Another run from the Busiek era of Avengers makes the tally, this one the Kang epic to end all Kang epics: an all-out assault by the world's would-be time-traveling conqueror, with the Avengers on the front line!

Collected in *Avengers Assemble Vol. 5 TPB*

57 Amazing Spider-Man #129

Who is this tough-as-nails vigilante bent on assassinating our friendly neighborhood Spidey? Why that would be Frank Castle, making his very first appearance as the Punisher!

Collected in *Marvel Masterworks: The Amazing Spider-Man Vol. 13*

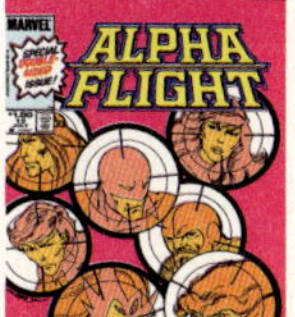

56 Alpha Flight (1983) #12

John Byrne shocked the world—especially the part of it north of the U.S. border—with the tragic death of longtime Alpha Flight commander Guardian.

Collected in *Alpha Flight Classic Vol. 2 TPB*

55 World War Hulk

World War Hulk #1-5

In this senses-shattering sequel to *Planet Hulk*, John Romita Jr. and Greg Pak deliver on the Hulk's revenge fantasy against an Earth that betrayed him. The green-skinned goliath has never been unleashed like this!

Collected in *World War Hulk TPB*

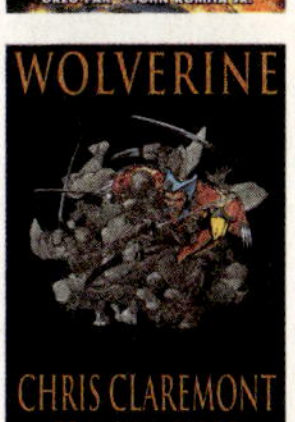

54 Wolverine by Chris Claremont & Frank Miller

Wolverine (1982) #1-4

Frank Miller, Chris Claremont, Wolverine and ninjas was more than X-Men fans of the early '80s could have asked for. What they got was every bit the classic an assembly like that could promise, with a Japan-based story that added exciting new dimensions to the saga of Wolverine.

Collected in *Wolverine by Claremont & Miller TPB*

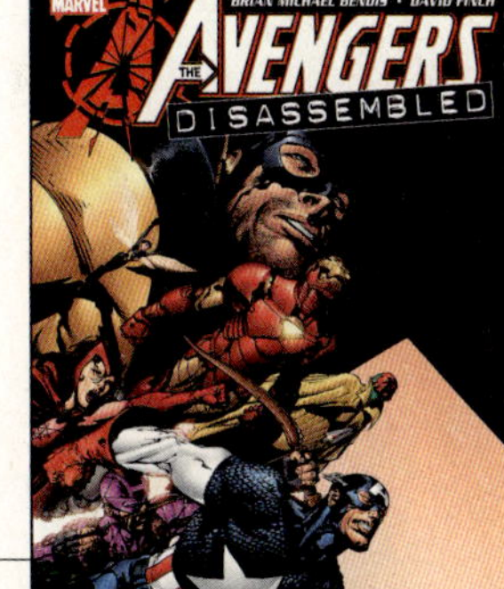

53 Avengers Disassembled

Avengers (1963) #500-503, Avengers Finale #1

This is it, the fountainhead from which much of the post-2004 narrative of the Marvel Universe has flowed. Brian Michael Bendis brought terror to Avengers Mansion, and David Finch made it look oh so beautiful. Lives were lost, and the direction of Earth's Mightiest Heroes was forever changed.

Collected in *Avengers Disassembled TPB*

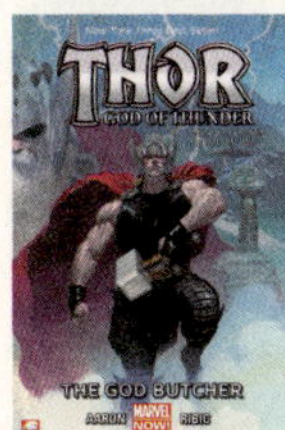

52 Thor: God of Thunder by Jason Aaron & Esad Ribic

Thor: God of Thunder #1-11

Past, present and future Thors are put to the test against the God Butcher, a nihilistic force bent on killing every immortal he can get his tendrils around. Aaron and Ribic bring their A-game to a new era of Thor.

Collected in *Thor: God of Thunder Vol. 1: The God Butcher* and *Vol. 2: Godbomb TPB*

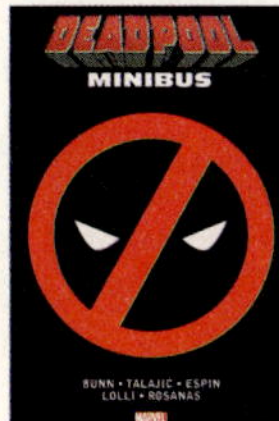

51 Deadpool Kills

Deadpool Kills the Marvel Universe #1-4, Deadpool Killustrated #1-4, Deadpool Kills Deadpool #1-4

Cullen Bunn's "Killogy" features Deadpool as you've never seen him, slaughtering his way across the Marvel Universe, slaying some of the most cherished characters in literature and then—of course, because it's so Wade Wilson—killing multiple alternate-reality versions of himself.

Collected in *Deadpool Minibus HC;* and *Deadpool Kills the Marvel Universe TPB, Deadpool Killustrated TPB* and *Deadpool Kills Deadpool TPB*

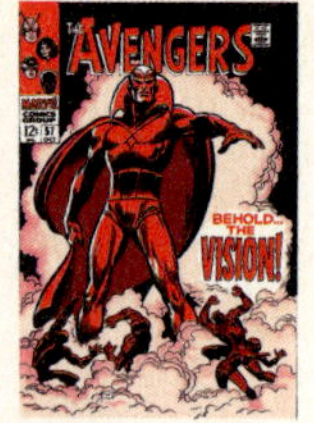

50 Avengers (1963) #57

Comics simply do not come as poetically beautiful as "Behold...the Vision!" by Roy Thomas and John Buscema, a classic highlighted by the first appearance of the Avenging android.

Collected in *Marvel Masterworks: The Avengers Vol. 6*

49 Hawkeye by Matt Fraction & David Aja

Hawkeye #1-21, Annual #1

Arguably the most endearing book from recent-vintage Marvel, Fraction and Aja place "Hawkguy" in a Brooklyn apartment building where he becomes a neighborhood champion. An Eisner Award-winning showcase for Clint Barton—but no less so for co-star Kate Bishop and a rescue dog named Lucky, aka Pizza Dog.

Collected in *Hawkeye Vol. 1: My Life as a Weapon, Vol. 2: Little Hits, Vol. 3: L.A Woman* and *Vol. 4: Rio Bravo TPB*

48 Giant-Size X-Men #1

The All-New, All-Different X-Men burst forth into the Marvel Universe in this instant classic by Len Wein and Dave Cockrum. Featuring the first assemblage of Wolverine, Banshee, Storm, Colossus, Nightcrawler and Thunderbird, the new team is sent on a death-defying mission to save Cyclops and the classic X-Men.

Collected in *Marvel Masterworks: The Uncanny X-Men Vol. 1*

47 The Korvac Saga

Avengers (1963) #170-177

Jim Shooter presages his *Secret Wars* with this all-time Avengers classic pitting the Avengers and the Guardians of the Galaxy against the cosmic might of Korvac.

Collected in *Avengers: The Korvac Saga TPB*

46 Amazing Spider-Man #700

The master plan in the making for one hundred issues comes to fruition, as Dr. Octopus' "Dying Wish" comes true—but the death of Spider-Man is only the beginning. Writer Dan Slott and artist Humberto Ramos unveil the newest hero in town: Otto Octavius, the Superior Spider-Man!

Collected in *Spider-Man: Dying Wish TPB*

45 Astonishing X-Men by Joss Whedon & John Cassaday

Astonishing X-Men #1-24, Giant-Size Astonishing X-Men #1

A saga so astonishing the whole run makes the list! Whedon and Cassaday achieved countless moments of perfection, including the emotional return of Colossus.

Collected in *Astonishing X-Men by Joss Whedon & John Cassaday Ultimate Collection Books 1-2 TPB*

44 Amazing Spider-Man (1999) #36

The day was 9/11, and the Twin Towers of the World Trade Center were brought down by acts of unspeakable evil...and there was nothing Spider-Man could do about it. J. Michael Straczynski and John Romita Jr. ruminate about the feelings of helplessness—and acts of heroism—brought about by the terrible events of that day.

Collected in *Amazing Spider-Man by JMS Ultimate Collection Book 1 TPB*

43 Amazing Spider-Man (1963) #50

"Spider-Man No More!" With so much responsibility surrounding his life as a wall-crawling hero, it was inevitable Peter Parker would face the ultimate crisis of faith: Can he remain Spider-Man? The answer in this issue, according to Stan Lee and John Romita Sr., is a tragic "no."

Collected in *Marvel Masterworks: The Amazing Spider-Man Vol. 5*

42 The Ultimates #1

The Ultimate line had already struck gold with updated versions of Spider-Man and the X-Men. There was only one place to go after that: Earth's Mightiest Heroes! Mark Millar and Bryan Hitch introduced Captain America and Iron Man to the fold in this widescreen first issue.

Collected in *The Ultimates Ultimate Collection TPB*

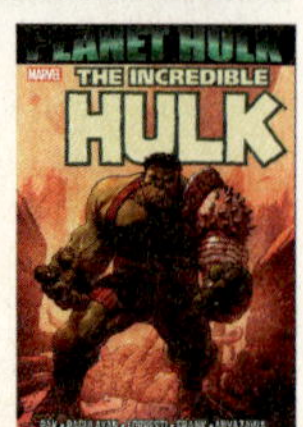

41 Planet Hulk

Incredible Hulk #92-105

Hulk epics do not get any more epic than this! Writer Greg Pak exiles the Jade Giant to a far-flung planet—courtesy of the Illuminati—where he gathers a band of compatriots on his journey from slave to king and finally, in the aftermath of ultimate tragedy, Earth's worst nightmare.

Collected in *Hulk: Planet Hulk TPB*

40 Fantastic Four #285

One of the gems of *Secret Wars II* is this poignant lesson in what it means to be a hero in the face of tragedy. For more than two decades, Johnny Storm had played the part of Sue's kid brother—but in this encounter with his ill-fated biggest fan and the Beyonder, the Human Torch was forced to grow up.

Collected in *Fantastic Four by John Byrne Omnibus Vol. 2*

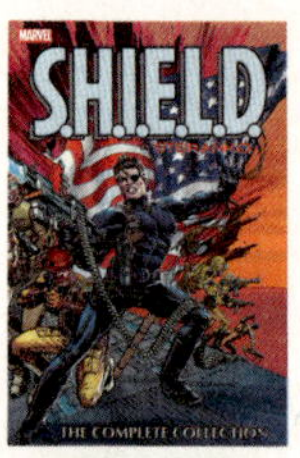

39 Captain America (2004) #25

Ed Brubaker's masterpiece continues with "The Death of Captain America," drawn by *Captain America* stalwart Steve Epting. Sharon Carter, the Falcon and all of America are plunged into chaos by the assassination of Steve Rogers.

Collected in *Captain America: The Death of Captain America Ultimate Collection TPB* and adapted in *Captain America: The Death of Captain America Prose Novel*

38 The Kree/Skrull War

Avengers (1963) #89-97

What does this seminal saga *not* have? Roy Thomas and Neal Adams pull out all the stops with cosmic warfare, Captain Marvel, Black Bolt and the Inhumans, Ant-Man's "fantastic voyage" inside the Vision, the return of Marvel's greatest Golden Age heroes, and...Skrull cows!

Collected in *Avengers: Kree/Skrull War TPB*

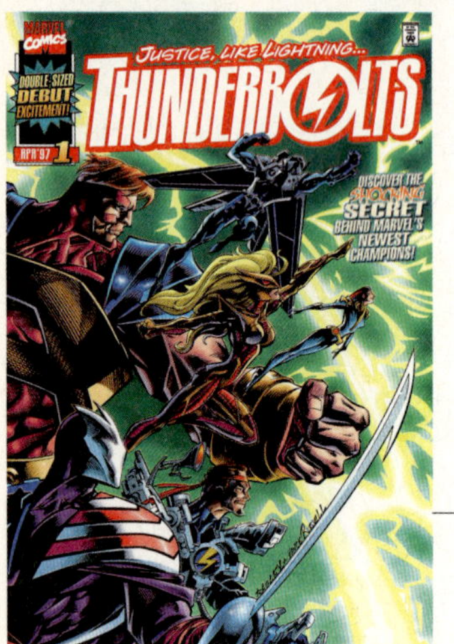
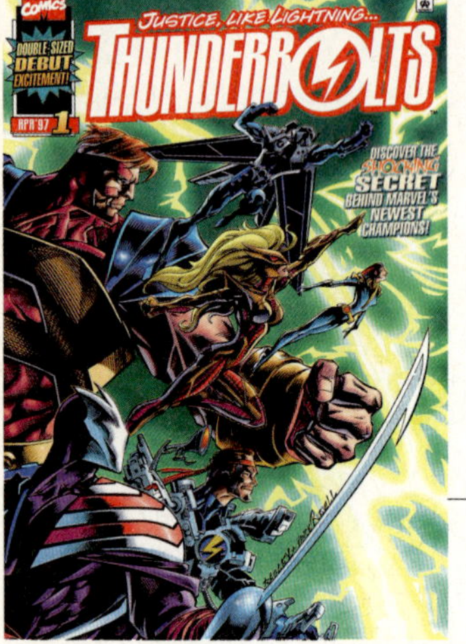

37 Thunderbolts (1997) #1

Arguably the most surprising last-page reveal in Marvel history (SPOILERS!!!). Kurt Busiek and Mark Bagley started a sensation with this tale of a vacuum of heroes being filled by opportunistic villains. Can evil save the day?

Collected in *Thunderbolts Classic Vol. 1 TPB*

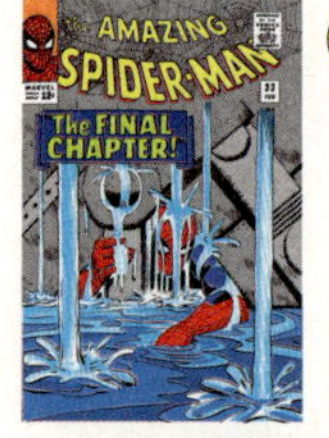

36 Nick Fury: Agent of S.H.I.E.L.D. by Steranko

Strange Tales #151-168; Nick Fury Agent of S.H.I.E.L.D. #1-3, #5

Marvel's hard-nosed super spy starred in some of the coolest, sleekest, most cutting-edge comics of the '60s thanks to writer/artist extraordinaire Jim Steranko. The Marvel Age of Comics did not get any hipper than this!

Collected in *S.H.I.E.L.D. by Steranko: The Complete Collection TPB*

35 Amazing Spider-Man (1963) #31-33

This timeless throwdown between Spidey and the mysterious Master Planner (now who could that be?) had the highest stakes imaginable for our hero: the life of Aunt May. Featuring the most iconic moment of "great power" from the early days of Spider-Man, "If This Be My Destiny!' remains a Lee/Ditko masterpiece.

Collected in *Marvel Masterworks: The Amazing Spider-Man Vol. 3*

34 Ultron Unlimited

Avengers (1998) #19-22

The Avengers were ascendant in the late '90s thanks to Kurt Busiek and George Perez. They also unleashed the deadliest iteration of Ultron yet, poised to commit global genocide and rebuild Earth in his own robotic image!

Collected in *Avengers Assemble Vol. 2 TPB*

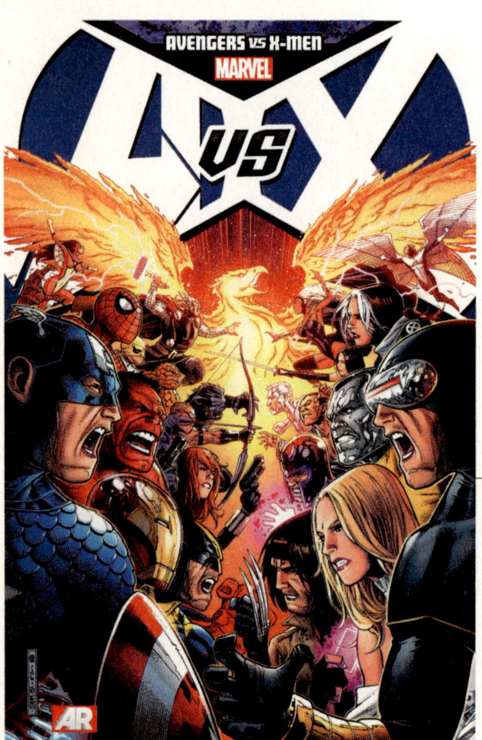

33 Avengers vs. X-Men

Avengers vs. X-Men #0-12

Cyclops will go to any lengths to keep Hope from harm, even if it means taking on the power of the Phoenix itself. With the mutant messiah caught in the middle, a deadly clash erupts between the X-Men and Avengers—and Professor X pays the ultimate price!

Collected in *Avengers vs. X-Men TPB*

32 X-Men: Fatal Attractions

X-Factor #92, X-Force #25, Uncanny X-Men #304, X-Men (1991) #25, Wolverine #75, Excalibur #71

In one of the biggest "wow" moments in Wolverine's history, Magneto did the unthinkable and stripped the Adamantium from Logan's skeleton. Andy Kubert's visuals and Xavier's stunning response paved the way for Onslaught.

Collected in *X-Men: Fatal Attractions HC*

31 Thor #337

Walter Simonson writes, draws and inks a Thor classic! Reinvigorating a moribund series with a fearless new take on Asgard, Simonson—and his ace in the hole, letterer John Workman—introduced a new hammer wielder by the name of Beta Ray Bill!

Collected in *Thor by Walter Simonson Vol. 1 TPB*

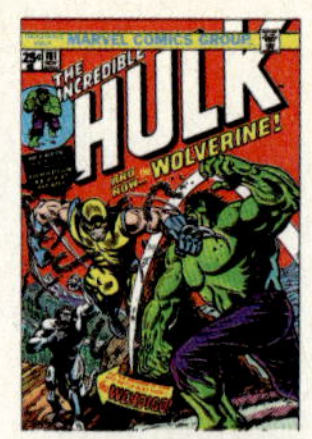

30 Incredible Hulk #181

A new hero crashes a fight in the Canadian wilderness between the Hulk and Wendigo in this story by writer Len Wein and artist Herb Trimpe. His name was Wolverine, and he was never heard from again.
Collected in *Marvel Masterworks: The X-Men Vol. 8*

29 Extremis

Iron Man (2005) #1-6

A more important, more durable, more definitive tale from Marvel's modern era can't be found on this list. Warren Ellis and Adi Granov not only reinvented the look and feel of the Iron Man armor, but also redefined the man inside—thrilling readers and setting the stage for Marvel's worldwide box-office takeover.
Collected in *Iron Man: Extremis TPB* and adapted in *Iron Man: Extremis Prose Novel*

28 Spider-Man: Blue

Spider-Man: Blue #1-6

Part of Jeph Loeb and Tim Sale's "color series" along with *Daredevil: Yellow* and *Hulk: Gray*, this sensitively told and lovingly drawn and colored story recaptures the innocence and tragedy of Peter Parker's love affair with Gwen Stacy.
Collected in *Jeph Loeb & Time Sale: Yellow, Blue & Gray HC and Spider-Man: Blue TPB*

27 Maximum Carnage

Spider-Man Unlimited #1-2, Web of Spider-Man #101-103, Amazing Spider-Man #378-380, Spider-Man #35-37, Spectacular Spider-Man #201-203

Cletus Kasady is off his leash in this Spider-Man mega-event. Joined on a killing spree by Doppelganger, Carrion and Demogoblin, Carnage can only be brought down by the combined efforts of Spider-Man and a team of heroes that includes Captain America, Deathlok and Venom. Wait a second...Venom is one of the good guys?
Collected in *Spider-Man: Maximum Carnage TPB*

26 House of M

House of M #1-8

From the rubble of Avengers Mansion in the aftermath of Avengers Disassembled, Brian Michael Bendis built the House of M, an alternate reality brought about by an insane Scarlet Witch. The climax of this pivotal tale in Marvel history comes with her three simple words: "No more mutants."
Collected in *House of M TPB*

25 The Death of Captain Marvel

Marvel Graphic Novel #1

Marvel inaugurated its line of tabloid-sized graphic novels with Jim Starlin's elegant, elegiac tribute to Mar-Vell in the last courageous battle of his life. A remarkable entry on this list not just for its storytelling, but also because the death has lasted.
Collected in *Captain Marvel: The Death of Captain Marvel TPB*

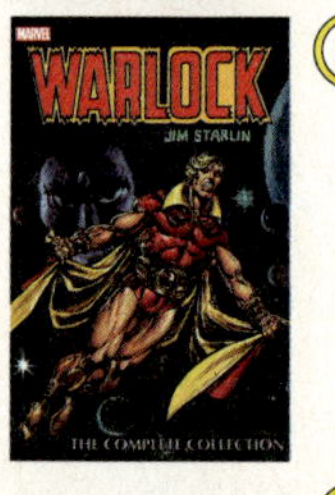

24 Warlock by Jim Starlin

Strange Tales #178-181, Warlock #9-15

Having already spanned the stars with Captain Marvel, Jim Starlin upped the ante by exploring the scope of the soul with Warlock. This self-contained epic has it all: the Infinity Gems; Thanos; and a classic team-up with Spider-Man, the Thing and the Avengers!
Collected in *Warlock by Jim Starlin: The Complete Collection TPB*

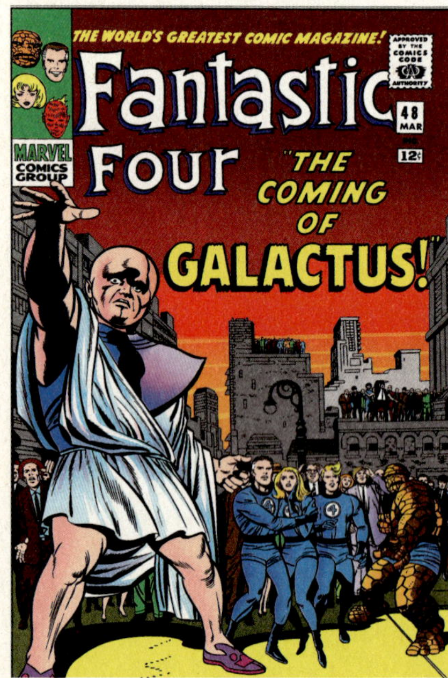

23 The Galactus Trilogy

Fantastic Four (1961) #48-50

A complex morality play that introduced Galactus and the Silver Surfer to the lexicon, "The Galactus Trilogy" was the Lee/Kirby saga that let comics readers know once and for all that Marvel was playing for keeps.
Collected in *Marvel Masterworks: The Fantastic Four Vol. 5*

22 Age of Apocalypse

For four months in 1995, X-Universe titles were replaced by limited series set in this alternate reality. Despite the continuity chaos—perhaps even because of it—this undeniably impactful saga and creative high point in X-Men gave rise to a world that found mutants ascendant. The only problem: It was a world ruled by Apocalypse.
Collected in *X-Men: The Complete Age of Apocalypse Epic Books 1-4 TPB*

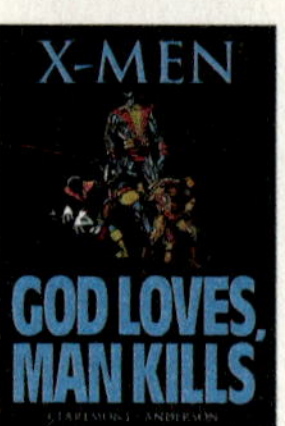

21 X-Men: God Loves, Man Kills

Marvel Graphic Novel #5

An evergreen story from the middle years of Chris Claremont's run, this beautifully rendered work by artist Brent Anderson and colorist Steve Oliff belied the tragedy at the heart of the tale as William Stryker led a crusade of hate against the X-Men.
Collected in *X-Men: God Loves, Man Kills TPB*

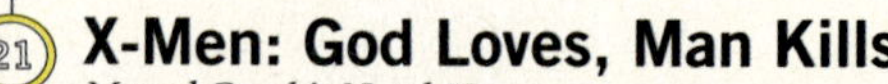

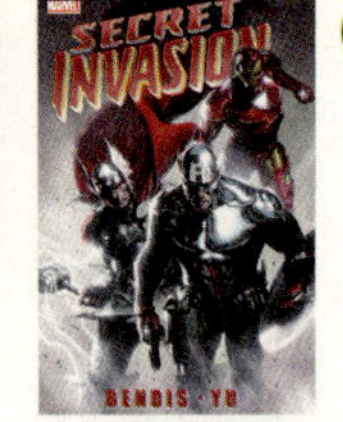

20 Secret Invasion

Secret Invasion #1-8

Who do you trust? In 2008, no one could be trusted thanks to a shape-shifting Skrull invasion that took over some of the most well-placed heroes in the Marvel Universe. The tension brought to bear by Brian Michael Bendis and Leinil Francis Yu produced one of the most thrilling crossover events in Marvel history.

Collected in *Secret Invasion TPB*

19 Daredevil #181

Frank Miller's run on *Daredevil* had brought pain and misery to the Man Without Fear, but the death of Elektra at the hands of his archenemy Bullseye would push him to the darkest depths of all.

Collected in *Daredevil by Frank Miller & Klaus Janson Vol. 1 TPB*

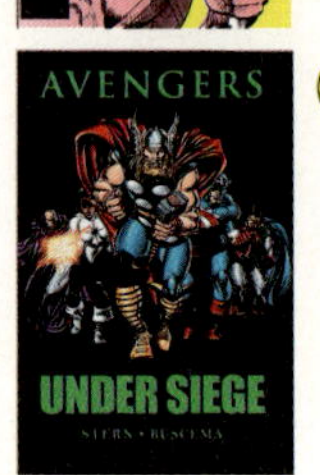

18 Avengers: Under Siege

Avengers #270-277

Baron Zemo's Masters of Evil truly lived up to their name in Roger Stern's harrowing narrative. Never before had the Avengers faced as excruciating a defeat—but never before had they risen up from such depths to claim victory. The art team of John Buscema and Tom Palmer gave this story a classically epic touch.

Collected in *Avengers: Under Siege Premiere HC*

17 The Kid Who Collected Spider-Man

Amazing Spider-Man #248

It was just a backup story, but Roger Stern and Ron Frenz's tale of true heroism touched the hearts of all who read it. Keep a box of tissues handy for this one!

Collected in *Spider-Man by Roger Stern Omnibus*

16 Annihilation

A sprawling cosmic epic spread across series starring Drax the Destroyer, Nova, Silver Surfer, Super-Skrull and Ronan the Accuser, *Annihilation* was the masterpiece that kick-started a cosmic revival at Marvel!

Collected in *Annihilation Omnibus*

15 Hulk (1962) #1

Lee and Kirby borrow the form of an Atlas Era monster and give him the function of a complex hero for the Marvel Age: The rage of weakling Bruce Banner begets the world-crushing, gamma-goliath known as the Incredible Hulk!

Collected in *Marvel Masterworks: The Incredible Hulk Vol. 1*

14 Fantastic Four (1961) #1

Reed Richards, Susan Storm, Johnny Storm and Ben Grimm ride a rocket into the cosmic firmament—that sound you hear is the ignition of the Marvel Age, and comics would never be the same!

Collected in *Marvel Masterworks: The Fantastic Four Vol. 1*

13 Captain America Comics #1

Joe Simon! Jack Kirby! The first appearance of Captain America! Hitler gets punched in the face! This one's got it all!

Collected in *Marvel Masterworks: Golden Age Captain America Vol. 1*

12 Avengers (1963) #1

All Loki wanted to do was beat his brother! He never suspected his machinations would create the greatest fighting force the world has ever known. Thor! Iron Man! Hulk! Ant-Man! The Wasp! These are Earth's Mightiest Heroes!

Collected in *Marvel Masterworks: The Avengers Vol. 1*

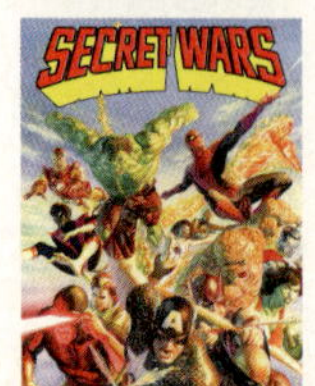

11 Secret Wars

Marvel Super Heroes Secret Wars #1-12

The cream of Marvel's heroes on one side, the worst of its villains on the other—now go fight! That simple recipe sure made for some big fun!

Collected in *Secret Wars TPB* and adapted in *Secret Wars Prose Novel*

HOT WHEELS®
CONGRATULATES
MARVEL
ON ITS
75TH
ANNIVERSARY!
WE'RE ALL REVVED UP AND
READY TO HIT THE FAST TRACK TOGETHER!
HOT WHEELS
MARVEL
75
YEARS

10 Amazing Fantasy #15

A young man learns the hard lesson that with great power, there must also come great responsibility in the iconic origin of Peter Parker and Spider-Man by Stan Lee and Steve Ditko.

Collected in *Marvel Masterworks: The Amazing Spider-Man Vol. 1*

09 The Winter Soldier

Captain America (2004) #1-14

They said Bucky would never return—*should* never return. But Ed Brubaker and Steve Epting did it, anyway, in one of the great Cap epics of all time that laid the groundwork for a pair of hit movies.

Collected in *Captain America: Winter Soldier Ultimate Collection TPB*

08 Marvels #1

Artist Alex Ross' photorealistic art enlivened writer Kurt Busiek's love letter to the Marvel Age of Comics, an evergreen gem from the early '90s.

Collected in *Marvels TPB* and *Marvels: The Platinum Edition HC Slipcase*

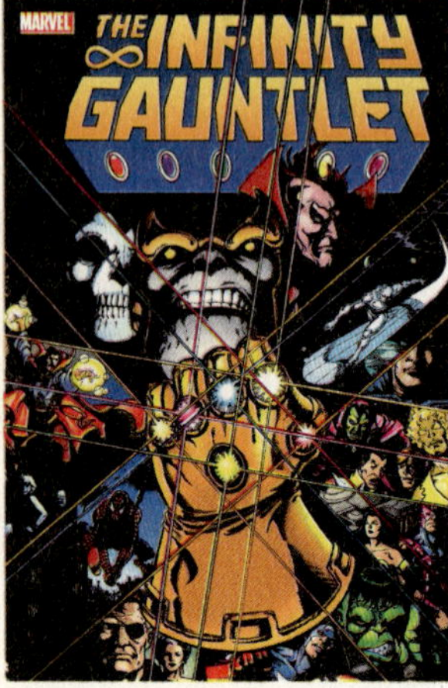

07 Infinity Gauntlet

Infinity Gauntlet #1-6

Thanos seeks universal power over mind, soul, space, time and reality through the Infinity Gems—and not even the cosmic heroes of the Marvel Universe can stop him!

Collected in *Infinity Gauntlet TPB* and *Infinity Gauntlet Omnibus*

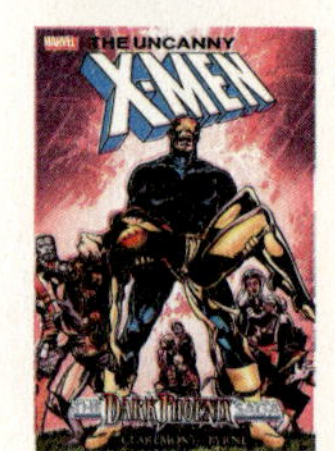

06 Days of Future Past

X-Men #141, Uncanny X-Men #142

The Sentinels rule in a dark, dystopian future. Mutantkind's only salvation is a trip to the past to change their fate, and the result is a Claremont/Byrne epic for the ages.

Collected in *X-Men: Days of Future Past TPB* and adapted in *X-Men: Days of Future Past Prose Novel*

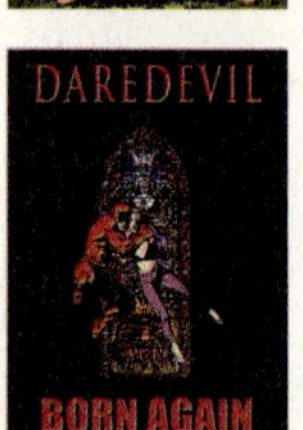

05 The Dark Phoenix Saga

X-Men #129-138

The Dark Phoenix has destroyed an entire planet, killing billions, and the Shi'ar Empire has issued the ultimate sanction: Jean Grey must die! Chris Claremont and John Byrne tell the seminal moment in X-Men history.

Collected in *X-Men: Dark Phoenix Saga TPB*

04 Born Again

Daredevil #227-231

Hailed as the definitive *Daredevil* storyline of all time, David Mazzucchelli draws Frank Miller's script of Daredevil's ultimate betrayal and utter destruction at the hands of the Kingpin.

Collected in *Daredevil: Born Again TPB*

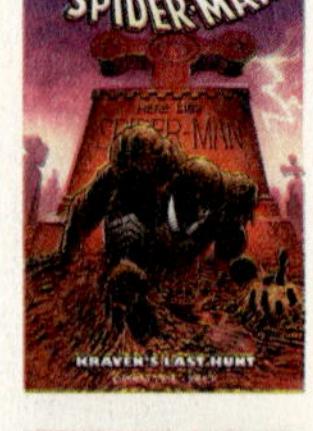

03 Kraven's Last Hunt

Amazing Spider-Man #293-294, Spectacular Spider-Man #131-132, Web of Spider-Man #31-32

Kraven has stalked every creature known to man, but the Spider has always eluded him. This high-stakes hunt ends in one of the most shocking deaths in Marvel history.

Collected in *Spider-Man: Kraven's Last Hunt TPB* and adapted in *Spider-Man: Kraven's Last Hunt Prose Novel*

02 Civil War

Civil War #1-7

The Marvel Universe is split down the middle as Iron Man and Captain America represent two sides of an ideological divide that will take all-out war to settle!

Collected in *Civil War TPB* and adapted in *Civil War Prose Novel*

01 The Death of Gwen Stacy

Amazing Spider-Man #121-122

The tragic death of Gwen Stacy proves that not even Peter Parker's great power and responsibility can protect the ones he loves—and enshrines the Green Goblin as Spidey Enemy No. 1.

Collected in *Spider-Man: Death of the Stacys TPB*

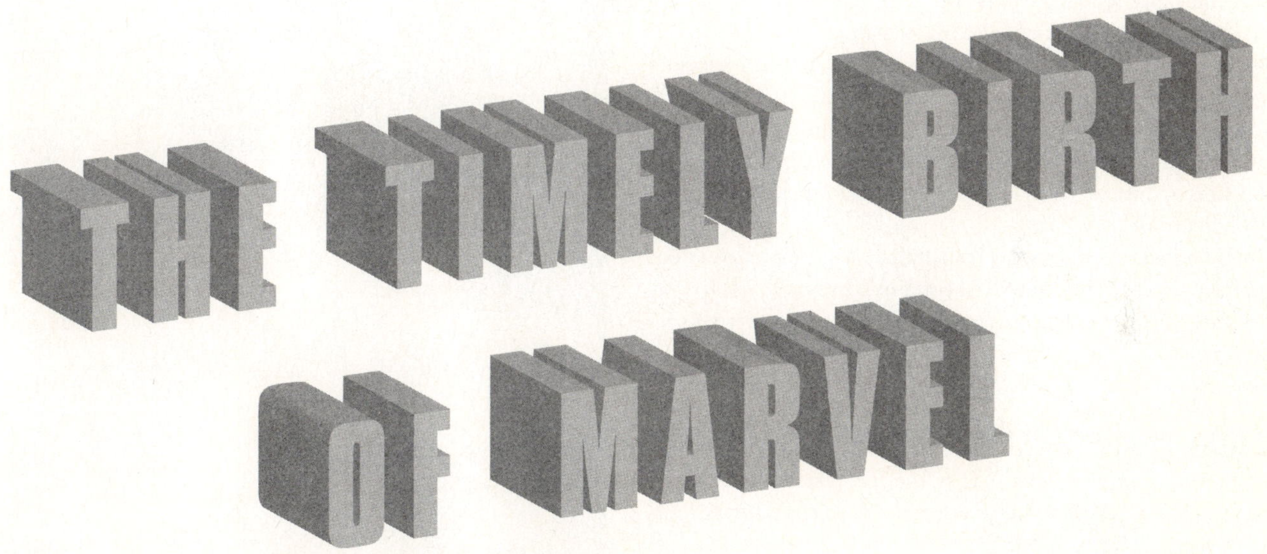

It started in 1939:
Inside the early evolution of Marvel Comics
under the stewardship of Stan Lee

By Robert Greenberger

There were heroes, but none of them were **super.**

Pulp magazines chronicling the fictional exploits of jungle heroes, police officers, private detectives, cowboys, soldiers of fortune and other he-men were filling newsstands across Depression-era America during the 1930s. Working as a salesman for Independent News, a distributor of such material, young Martin Goodman saw how successfully the pulps were selling, and left Independent with two others to form Columbia Publications and follow suit.

Borrowing money, he became his own boss in 1932, releasing *Western Supernovel Magazine* in May 1933. Dozens of titles followed. Goodman added *Ka-Zar* in 1936, his first pulp featuring a recurring character. In 1938, he introduced *Marvel Science Stories* — a science-fiction title — just as super heroes were transforming the nascent comic-book field.

Comic books, in the form we're familiar with today, had established themselves by 1935 and were being published by a variety companies, but no title had been successful enough to encourage others to join the field.

Until *Action Comics #1* and the arrival of Superman, that is.

THE RISE OF THE TIMELY SUPER HEROES

The following summer, Frank Torpey, the salesman for a company called Funnies Inc., approached Goodman with an opportunity. Funnies — whose ranks included artists Joe Simon, Bill Everett and Carl Burgos — packaged material to sell to publishers. Torpey reportedly showed Goodman super-hero titles from other publishers and suggested he add a comics line to remain competitive.

Goodman agreed and used the title *Marvel Comics* (October 1939) for his first release, tying in with the somewhat-related *Marvel Science Stories*. For that first issue, Everett contributed a story featuring his Sub-Mariner character; Burgos introduced the Human Torch, an android that could burst into flame; and Paul Gustavson created the Angel. The title, sporting Frank R. Paul's painted cover of the flame-covered Torch, sold out its 80,000-copy print run. A second printing quickly followed at ten times the size.

WE LOVE YOU, PATSY: **It wasn't all super heroes at Timely! In 1945, Stan & Co. produced a couple gals that are still active to this day at the House of Ideas, teen beauties Patsy Walker and Millie the Model. (Cover art to *Patsy Walker #1*.)**

Goodman decided to build his own staff rather than rely on a packager, so he recruited Joe Simon away from Funnies to become his first editor in chief. He named the comics division Timely Publications and planned to fill the racks with his company's creations.

Marvel Comics became *Marvel Mystery Comics* with the second issue, released just three months later at the beginning of 1940. In issue #4, Namor the Sub-Mariner took on the Nazi threat for the first time

— well before America entered World War II.

With war drums beating ever louder, Simon and Kirby decided Timely needed a patriotic hero readers could rally around. The result was *Captain America Comics #1*, released in March 1941.

By the summer, Goodman had launched *Red Raven Comics #1*, his first title named for a single character. The issue also included a story featuring the initial Timely art by Jack Kirby. Simon and Kirby had met earlier when both worked for Fox Comics, and they struck up a partnership. *Red Raven*'s sales were poor; it was renamed *Human Torch Comics* with the second issue, providing the young company with its first spinoff. That issue also introduced Toro, a human teen sidekick for the Torch who could likewise burst into flame. As the year progressed, the first incarnations of Marvel Boy and the Vision also made their debuts.

STAN LEE ON THE SCENE

Before the year was out, Goodman decided Simon needed editorial help and hired his wife's cousin's son, Stanley Lieber. The 17-year-old had wanted to be a writer, and this was the opportunity of a lifetime.

"It was exciting for me," Lee recalls. "It was my first job in a publishing office, which was very glamorous. Simon was the boss, but it was really Simon, Kirby and me. Goodman told them what to do.

"It was thrilling. I was just 17 but felt like a professional. I didn't talk to the other writers and artists that much."

With war drums beating ever louder, Simon and Kirby decided Timely needed a patriotic hero around whom readers could rally. The result was *Captain America Comics #1*, released in March 1941. The cover depicted Cap punching Adolf Hitler, which told readers all they needed to know. The title was a smashing success.

For the third issue, Simon gave Lieber his first text-page assignment. Reserving his birth name for when he became a "real" writer, he signed it "Stan Lee."

With super heroes in ascension, Goodman recognized he had three hits on his hands. He used Cap, Sub-Mariner and the Torch repeatedly — first in *All Winners Comics* and eventually in their own titles. Bucky Barnes, Cap's sidekick, and Toro led a team of young heroes in *Young Allies Comics*. Other costumed heroes turning up included the Destroyer, Whizzer and Jack Frost (Stan's first creation). None matched the popularity of the first three.

The first major crossover in comics history occurred that fall. *Human Torch Comics #5* included a book-length story featuring a knockdown battle between the Torch and the Sub-Mariner. Legend has it Everett oversaw the creation of the 64-page story over a single weekend by filling his apartment with about a dozen artists.

Despite their success, Simon and Kirby quit staff as 1941 wound down over a dispute with Goodman.

"Goodman asked me to look after things while he looked for an older and more seasoned editor," Lee says. "He never hired anyone. That's when I started talking to the artists and writers."

Just after America entered the war, titles featuring humor and funny animals were among the top sellers for other companies. Goodman ordered *Joker Comics*, which premiered in April 1942 and featured Basil Wolverton's Powerhouse Pepper, followed in July with *Krazy Komics*, which starred Ziggy Pig and Silly Seal. Later in the year, *Comedy Comics* arrived. That year, Stan enlisted and left staff for the duration of the war. Vince Fago, Stan's artist on Ziggy Pig, took over as editor.

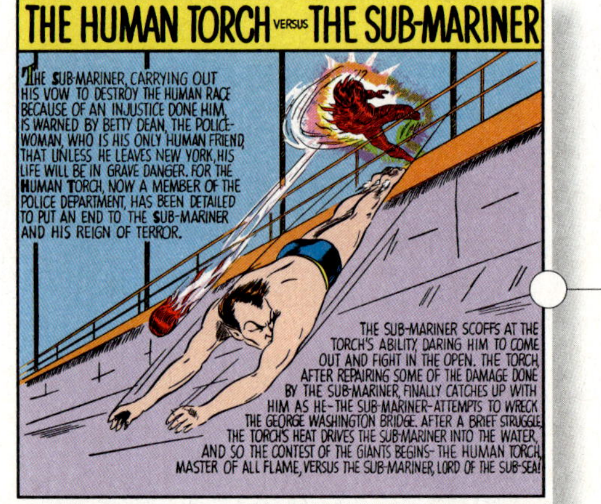

A BATTLE FOR THE AGES:
Timely holds the honor of the first character crossover, when a battle between the Human Torch and Namor the Sub-Mariner raged over two issues of Marvel Mystery Comics. (Art from MMC #9 by Bill Everett and Carl Burgos.)

The following year, Super Rabbit arrived in *Comedy Comics #14*, quickly becoming the title's cover feature and one of Timely's most successful characters. Meanwhile, super heroes came and went with surprising regularity as few connected with readers. The first major heroine, Miss America, didn't arrive until her debut in November 1943's *Marvel Mystery Comics #49*. She earned her own title just a few months later, the same month Ziggy got his.

Miss America #2 featured the first appearance of Ruth Atkinson's Patsy Walker, who was so popular she pushed Miss America out of her own book. Tastes were changing, and Goodman renamed a number of titles — such as *Amazing Comics*, which became *Complete Comics* — and filled the pages of each with the next great fad.

POST-WAR BLUES

As the war wound down in 1945, readers' tastes became harder to gauge. Heroes were rapidly being retired, and more teen humor arrived in the form of *Georgie, Nellie the Nurse* and *Millie the Model. Millie* proved a durable feature, lasting well into the 1970s. And as the war ended, Stan received his military discharge and returned to staff, while Fago went back to the drawing board. "Things felt differently," Lee says. "But I got right back into it."

Goodman continued to mix and match his product offerings — a full slate of super heroes, funny animals, humor and teen humor. The Blonde Phantom arrived in 1946, and the most popular heroes teamed up as the All-Winners Squad in *All Winners Comics #19*.

Several noteworthy artists did their first Timely work that year — including a young Gene Colan and war veteran Harvey Kurtzman, who produced a tremendous amount of material during his three years with the company. His "Hey Look!" feature debuted in *Jeanie Comics #17* more than a year after he drew the first installment.

Goodman dropped the Timely name from his covers, briefly sampling "A Marvel Magazine" as a replacement, but later choosing to go without a company name.

Cap had Bucky and the Torch had Toro, but Sub-Mariner didn't have a partner until Namora's arrival in 1947's *Marvel Mystery Comics #82*. Her debut signaled an attempt to find other heroines to whom readers would respond, although none matched the success of Patsy and Millie. *Sub-Mariner Comics* was renamed *Official True Crime Cases* as crime narratives became more popular that year, and

MARVEL'S "BIG THREE" OF THE GOLDEN AGE: CAPTAIN AMERICA, HUMAN TORCH & SUB-MARINER

The start of the modern-day Marvel Universe and its part in the rise in popularity of super heroes can be traced back to Marvel's Golden Age "Big Three": Sub-Mariner, Human Torch and Captain America.

The Sub-Mariner (aka Prince Namor) was Marvel's first super hero. Created by Bill Everett, Namor was a half-human, half-Atlantean hybrid with superhuman strength and reflexes. Unlike other Golden Age heroes, Namor was unique in that he was far from an all-American role model. The young prince was hot-blooded and had a hair-trigger temper, easily making him one of comics' first anti-heroes. He wasn't afraid to attack surface-dwelling humans if they threatened his home — even if that meant rampaging in New York City and fighting one of Marvel's other heroes, the Human Torch. He softened during the wartime years, teaming up with democratic governments and other superhumans to fight the Axis powers.

The Human Torch was featured on the cover of *Marvel Comics #1*, and for good reason: Carl Burgos' blazing icon was sure to catch any reader's eye. Very different from the Fantastic Four's Johnny Storm — who would inherit the moniker in 1961 — the original Human Torch was an android created by Professor Phineas T. Horton. The Torch was initially a blank slate, learning the functions of human society while fighting crime. Like many other Golden Age heroes, he later gained a sidekick: Toro (Thomas Raymond), a young man with similar powers to his once-naive android mentor. It was only natural that the Human Torch and Toro would help save the world by taking the fight to Europe and the Pacific.

You can't talk about the Golden Age without including Captain America in the conversation. Joe Simon and Jack Kirby's legendary hero is one of the great icons of American culture. To combat Nazi Germany, the American government turned weakling Steve Rogers into the red-white-and-blue clad Sentinel of Liberty. Cap possessed enhanced strength and speed and wielded a bulletproof shield he could sling with uncanny accuracy. Joined by young sidekick Bucky Barnes, Cap smashed the Axis time and again. Cap was also one of the few heroes to have an enduring nemesis during the wartime era: the sinister Nazi agent known as the Red Skull. Everything that made Captain America iconic during the 1940s, particularly his all-American charisma and leadership skills, remains integral to the character today.

These three heroes would join forces in Marvel's first super-hero team, the All-Winners Squad in *All Winners Comics #19* and *#21* after the conclusion of World War II. Though interest in super heroes waned enough for the Big Three to drop out of publication for a time, all three were revived briefly during the fifties' Atlas Era. Captain America's Commie-smasher persona was a bracing change from the Nazi-fighting Cap of World War II and would eventually be explained as a separate character — later to become a nemesis of Steve Rogers. During the Silver Age, Cap was revived from suspended animation to lead a new team of heroes, the Avengers, and the Sub-Mariner became a long-running supporting character in *Fantastic Four.* In the seventies, Marvel writer/editor Roy Thomas's interest in Golden Age comics led him to reintroduce the All-Winners Squad in the form of the Invaders, which has kept these Golden Age heroes alive and well.

— MICHAEL AND NATHAN KRONENBERG

Wacky Duck became *Justice.*

Fawcett was known for Captain Marvel and DC for Superman, but Goodman's now-nameless company had no signature character around which to build a line. It was a company without an identity. Goodman continued to sample genres, adding Western titles such as *Two-Gun Kid* and *Kid Colt* in 1948. Namora received her own title — as did the goddess of love, *Venus.* Also appealing to female readers was Goodman's entry into romance comics with *My Romance #1.*

The day of the super hero was coming to an end, and Goodman slowly wound down their titles. *Captain America* became *Captain America's Weird Tales*; by the final issue in February 1950, Cap was absent from the book altogether. Instead, Goodman was flooding the field with romance titles, from *Love Dramas* to *Cowboy Romances.*

Lee now was acting as both editor in chief and art director. "I realized how important artwork was in doing comic books," he says. "As I stayed there longer and longer, I studied the art form, trained my eyes. I began to learn which drawings the reader would enjoy. Which told the story best? Which detracted from the experience? I never asked for a change without explaining why, so he understood what I meant. By then, we all spoke the same language.

"There was a time I was in reception when an artist came in, an older man in his late 40s. I was about 18 at the time, and he walked in and said, 'Hey kid, I'd like to see Mr. Lee.' I knew he'd be embarrassed to see it was me. I asked him to wait for a minute. I didn't know how to handle it. I think I said he was busy at the time."

Lee never had trouble finding talent for his growing and ever-changing lineup of titles. "Most of the guys were so versatile, they could do almost anything," he says. "I always tried to find work for them. If it was an adventure-strip artist, and I needed something different, maybe I'd have him ink it so we didn't let him go. Some didn't have the style we needed, and that was a part of the business.

"I loved doing the stories. Sometimes an artist would come in and want to do a detective story. If I didn't have any, I'd offer him something close. Here's a Western — instead of saying 'Follow that car,' they say 'Follow that stagecoach.' A story is a story, that's the way I felt about it. I think I'm the ultimate hack writer — give me something to write, I just love writing anything."

DAWN OF A NEW DECADE: THE ATLAS ERA

As 1950 arrived, the medium fell under attack by groups fearing the material was either too juvenile, too explicit or too violent. Comics were being burned, and sales were deteriorating, which forced many publishers out of the field. Others held on — including Goodman, who had by then dumped his pulp magazines for other fictional magazines such as men's adventure books and true confessions. He continued to flood the newsstands with offerings for every conceivable taste, including comics that blended genres such as *Cowgirl Romances.* As America became involved in the Korean War, a new genre emerged. Soon, war titles were challenging the weird mystery comics — as noted by the debuts in 1951 of *Strange Tales #1* and *Combat Kelly #1,* the first war title to focus on a central character.

The year ended with Goodman creating his own distribution company: Atlas. By December, all his titles carried the Atlas symbol, ushering in a new era — even though the company was never formally renamed.

Goodman and Lee continued to experiment with offbeat ideas such as *Sports Action* and *Lorna the Jungle Queen.* Now controlling his destiny from editorial through the newsstand, Goodman cranked out more and more material — reaching 400 releases in 1952, a pinnacle for the era.

JOE MANEELY'S BLACK KNIGHT:
Artist Maneely might have been Stan Lee's right-hand man during the Marvel Age of Comics had he not passed away at such an untimely age. His art on Black Knight was reprinted in Marvel Masterworks: Black Knight/Yellow Claw Vol. 1 HC. (Cover art to *Black Knight #5.*)

By this point, and well until 1966, Goodman lacked a breakout character capable of being heavily merchandised. Captain America came closest with a 1940s movie serial, but none of Goodman's properties sparkled brightly enough to catch the attention of toy and game manufacturers — or Hollywood.

While complaints about comics continued, Goodman brought back his Big Three in *Young Men #24* at the end of 1953; months later, Cap, Torch and Sub-Mariner would also return to their own titles. But the revivals proved exceedingly short-lived, although *Captain America Weird Tales* was graced with art by newcomer artist John Romita. *Sub-Mariner Comics* lasted the longest due to interest in developing him for television, but the plan fell through. Instead, Fredric Wertham's *Seduction of the Innocent*, a poorly researched and hysterical treatise on the negative influence of comics on children, topped the bestseller lists and cast a dark shadow over the entire field.

The Kefauver Hearings examined the causes of juvenile delinquency, and comics fell under their gaze. The industry formed the Comics Magazine Association of America, wrote a set of rules and began affixing the Comics Code Authority seal of approval to books that were devoid of gore, sex and any content that hinted at lack of

I WISH THERE WAS SOMETHING FUN TO DO.
HEY, GUYS! WHAT'S UP?
NOTHING REALLY...WE'RE BORED.
I KNOW! WE CAN PUT ON OUR SNEAKERS AND PLAY MARVEL SUPER HEROES!
YEAH! LET'S GO GET THEM!
COOL! BUT WHAT'S OUR MISSION?
CONGRATULATIONS TO...
MARVEL
75 YEARS!
THANK YOU FOR THE GREAT CUSTOM WORK!
MARVEL 75 YEARS
BE THE HERO! stride rite®
©2014 Marvel

respect for authority.

While other publishers faded away, Goodman and Lee made their books squeaky clean, forcing them to come up with some new titles. The year the Code arrived, so did *Black Knight* and *Rawhide Kid*. Trying for something new didn't always mean success: *Black Knight* gave way after five issues to *Yellow Claw*, a new take on a global menace owing more than a little to its pulp ancestors.

THE IMPLOSION

Goodman managed to keep the company afloat during these turbulent years, but it was a bleak decade for creators; many writers and artists left the field for other work.

The situation got even worse in 1957 when Goodman folded Atlas and signed with America's largest distributor, American News. By May, though, American News had folded and the arrangement collapsed, leaving Goodman scrambling to find a new home for his comics, magazines and paperback books. While he looked, he had Lee fire everyone and downsize the company, stopping talent in the middle of stories.

"It was the toughest thing in the world," Lee says. "You let the staff go, and by now they were friends of mine. I knew their families. Goodman went to Florida and left it to me to fire everyone."

Stan Goldberg, who joined the staff at 16 in 1949, was in charge of the in-house coloring department while drawing short stories for the horror titles. Like so many of those who lost their jobs, Goldberg drifted out of comics and went back to school.

Finally, Goodman made a deal with his former employer, Independent News — now the top distributor and home to the DC Comics line of titles. Limited to only eight titles a month, Goodman hedged his bets and reduced his entire line to sixteen bimonthly books. They were a mix of romance, Western, mystery and kid humor.

"I was only out of work for a few weeks when Stan called," Goldberg wrote in 1991. "They were going to start publishing again, and they needed someone to color the books. Stan wanted to do a teenage title, and I guess the old adage of being in the right place at the right time proves itself out. There I was, this young artist who only wanted to draw adventure, given a chance to draw cute teenagers. Ugh. I went home with my package of Dan DeCarlo, Al Hartley and Bob Oksner books. I've always respected these guys, and when I really got into the books, the drawings just knocked me out.

"Stan was a big, big influence on me in my new career. I would come to the office almost every day with pages of art, and Stan would be there to tear them apart."

KIRBY, DITKO, HECK AND LIEBER(S)

Lee had a few easy months as he used up inventory and then began to find an identity for each title. He first had to contend with the untimely death of his favorite artist, Joe Maneely. To fill the gap, Lee was fortunate to regain the services of Jack Kirby, who became available after a falling out with DC. Lee wrote just about everything, and he began to rely increasingly on Kirby, Steve Ditko, Don Heck and his brother, Larry Lieber, to fill his titles as 1958 wound down.

During the next year or two, Goodman let the line settle, making only tweaks rather than wholesale changes. Lee was able to establish solid working relationships with his artists as a result — especially Ditko, who turned out some of his finest work in the short tales that filled titles such as *Tales of Suspense* and *Tales to Astonish*. His art was subtle and atmospheric, vastly different from Kirby's energetic monster work. Lee created *Amazing Fantasy* as a home for Ditko's sophisticated stories.

By now, Lee had been writing for the company for nearly 20 years. He loved to write, and following the trends through various genres was satisfying up to a point. "I loved them all," he says. "I loved the variety and the fact that I didn't get stuck in one genre. I loved putting my name on every story. That became a problem with our romance books. They were first-person confessions, told by girls. I was very proud when I came up with 'As told to Stan Lee.'

Whereas Fawcett was known for Captain Marvel and DC for Superman, Goodman's now-nameless company really had no single character to build a line around.

"I loved doing the animated cartoons. I got to work with Al Jaffee, Dave Berg, some other great people.

"You know, Harvey Kurtzman was great. He could really lay out and tell a story. I was fortunate to have him. I got to work with so many talented people. There are only a few I missed out on. I can't remember all their names, but I know I always wanted to do something with Joe Kubert but never had the chance."

Still, Lee was growing more concerned with each passing year that comics might vanish entirely. He also wanted to write in other media and felt his chance might never come. While content with comics, he was beginning to yearn for something more.

The war books were soon gone, their slots taken either by new mysteries or female-centric books such as *A Date with Millie*. Goodman was cautious for a change, observing but not following trends. DC's revival of super heroes began in 1956, but it wasn't until 1961 that Goodman was ready to try his hand at anything super heroic.

So the Golden Age gave way to the Atlas Era, which gave way to... well, we all know what came next. It was fantastic, it was amazing, and it set the pace for a cultural revolution in comics. Stan Lee was about to launch the Marvel Age of Comics! •

HAPPY BIRTHDAY, MARVEL COMICS!

IT'S A MARVEL WORLD AND PANINI IS PROUD TO BE YOUR PARTNER SINCE 1994

THE 75TH ANNIVERSARY INTERVIEW

BY JOHN RHETT THOMAS

IT'S 2014, AND STAN IS STILL "THE MAN."

But 75 years ago, when Timely Comics bowed with *Marvel Comics #1*, he was 17-year-old Stanley Lieber. The recently hired Stan was working as an errand boy for the artists in the publisher's Manhattan office, but soon he'd be running the place—and the rest is comic-book history. The milestones in The Man's career would take far too long to recount here: his long tenure at Timely and Atlas during the '40s and '50s; his leading role ushering in Marvel's Silver Age of the '60s; his knack for dialogue that enlivened characters like Spider-Man, Captain America, Dr. Strange and, of course, the Fantastic Four; his long-running Spider-Man newspaper strip; and his role as ambassador for Marvel for more than 50 years—to name just a few. And heck, he polished off the introduction to George Romero's *Empire of the Dead* trade paperback just last week. Who says this still isn't the Marvel Age of Comics? Certainly not Stan, who visited with us for this wide-ranging interview in celebration of his tenure with the House of Ideas.

ROGERS
OLIVER
&
MORALES
2006
+JOSE
5TH AV
RADIO CITY
417

JOHN RHETT THOMAS:

Thanks for talking with us, Stan. We really appreciate it.

STAN:

And well you should. Now, what the hell is this all about?

JOHN RHETT THOMAS:

Well, Stan, this interview is all about you.

STAN:

Oh. I like that! *(Laughter.)*

STAN'S MIGHTIEST HEROES: Iron Man, Thor, Ant-Man/Giant-Man and the Wasp all had their own titles, while Captain America was fresh from an iceberg and Rick Jones was stuck with the Hulk! Put 'em all together and you've got one heckuva team: the Avengers!

It's Marvel's 75th Anniversary—the "diamond" anniversary—
(Interrupts.) So that means you're giving me a diamond, right? Where's my diamond?

***(Laughter.)* We can have one sent right over to you, Stan! But first, I have to ask: If this comic-book thing doesn't work out for you, do you have a backup plan?**
Yeah, I'm gonna be the only actor in the world who specializes in cameos.

You've got a great filmography so far! Let's talk about those movies: Marvel's *Iron Man*, *Thor*, *Captain America: The First Avenger*, *The Incredible Hulk*, *The Avengers*, and all their sequels and successors—up to and including last month's *Guardians of the Galaxy*. Arguably the most important thing the Marvel Cinematic Universe has done to spur its massive popularity is borrowing a concept you pushed to make the Marvel Age of Comics in the '60s such an enduring success: the idea of a shared universe—in which characters star in their own storylines, but also heavily interact with and influence each other.
It's amazing, isn't it? All the progress in special effects that have made these characters look so compelling on screen, and now they get their own movies that connect with each other. I can see why the audiences are thrilled by these movies. I hope I can keep up with all the cameos—otherwise, the whole thing falls apart!

What do you think of the Marvel Masterworks library? Marvel has been publishing these volumes since 1987, collecting all its classic comics from the Golden Age through the late '70s and early '80s.
Well, I love seeing them. I'm so impressed that these are referred to as Marvel Masterworks. You know, I think I made up that name.

You made up that name?
(Laughter.) I made up the name…

It's got two M's in it…
Yeah! I love those words that are, what's the term?

Alliterative.
Alliterative! Alliterative, of course. *(Laughter.)* And when I get those Marvel Masterworks, and I put them on the bookshelf at home, it's thrilling. It really is! All these things that I did a million years ago…

I know you've done a lot of work writing the introductions.
That seems to be my biggest thing today.

When I was a kid, the concept of having all the earliest Marvel Comics available to read was just an alien thought. It never occurred to me to even wish for it!
I never would have guessed this would happen in a million years—that years later people would be collecting these. If I had known, I would have collected them. I would have saved them!

I know, and you were in a position to save a lot of them, too! *(Laughter.)*
Can you take us back to your first days in the office, in 1940, when you were just a teenager?

What was that like?
I think it was in the McGraw-Hill Building, on the east side of Manhattan—I think 34th Street or so. It's hard for me to remember. It was a big green, glass building. The company was called Magazine Management, I think.

Comics were the least of what were being published at that time. They published pulp magazines, romance stories, adventure stories, men's magazines. I think they were trying to do a movie magazine. And then they had the comic department, and it was run by two guys: Joe Simon and Jack Kirby. They hired me as an assistant, but my job was really just to go down to the drugstore and get them sandwiches at lunchtime and to fill the inkwells. In those days, they used ink to draw the comics, and the inkwells had to always be filled. So I ran errands, erased the pages after they had been inked and did a little proofreading.

I was there for a few months, thinking this wasn't the greatest job in the world but it was good enough until I figured out what I wanted to do with my life. And then—for some reason I never fully understood—they were both fired. And I was the only guy left in the department. And Martin Goodman, who was the publisher, asked if I thought I could handle things until they found a grown-up.

Well, when you're 17 or so, what do you know? So I said, "Sure, I can do it!" And I guess he never got around to finding a grown-up because he never told me to stop doing what I was doing!

Well, one thing you had always said that struck me as funny was that you were saving your real name, Stanley Lieber, for when you were going to write the so-called Great American Novel. Technically, you never got around to writing a piece of prose that stood for that—but back in those early days, did you have anything in mind for what you wanted to write about?
Nothing at all.

Nothing at all?
In fact, even today I never know what I'm gonna write until I sit down to write it.

STAN IN THE SANCTUM SANCTORUM: Stan's meeting with Dr. Strange is gorgeously rendered by Alan Davis in the *Stan Lee Meets Doctor Strange* one-shot.

But I found out that I don't have the temperament to write books, 'cause I get very—I don't know whether "bored" is the word—I don't really like to write until I'm in the act of writing. When I start writing I get very interested in it—but if I know I have to write something, I'll put it off 'til the last minute. So I'm really a hack writer. I write something when it has to be written, and I usually wait 'til the last minute. And I could never write a novel, 'cause the thought of sitting and knowing I have three, four hundred pages to write—I'd never get started.

Now, friends of mine who are novelists have said to me, "Stan, you're a jerk. Just get an idea for a novel and write five pages a night! You could do that in a half-hour. And do that every night!" And they're right, but I can't do it. So I realize that I should have kept my own name, because comic writing is perfect for me—'cause I was able to write a book in a day, and then it was finished! Now the fact that I had to write another one the next day—I was too dumb to think of that. I just knew, "Boy, I wrote it fast, I'm finished! Great!" Next day was another project; I'd worry about that later. So I love things that I can write and finish by the time I get up from the typewriter—or now, the computer. If it takes an hour, two hours, three hours—the point is, it's finished by the time I go to sleep. And for some stupid reason I like that.

(Laughter.) You see, the reason was, I wanted to do something good, something memorable.

You could have written it about the human condition, or about war and peace...
No. To be brutally honest, I wasn't even thinking of anything that exotic. I was just thinking, "I'd like to write something that will sell, and it'll make me famous." And comics were so—I won't say hated—but were so disrespected in those days, most parents didn't even want their kids to read comics. If ever anybody over the age of twelve or thirteen was seen with a comic you'd think there was something wrong with him. People just had no respect at all for comics. So I felt, if I want to be a writer someday, I'd like to write a book! People respect people who write books. I didn't have any idea what I wanted to write about, and so I thought, "I'm gonna save my name"—and just jokingly—"for the Great American Novel."

Well, one of the important elements of a great novel—or any piece of literature that stands the test of time—is characterizations that readers can learn something from, and perhaps identify with and adapt into their own life. When you boil it down, it seems that you did, in essence, write at least that part of the Great American Novel with *Amazing Spider-Man*. The story of Peter Parker—how he went from a nobody to a hero of great power using his arachnid-like abilities responsibly to help others—fits in with this idea.

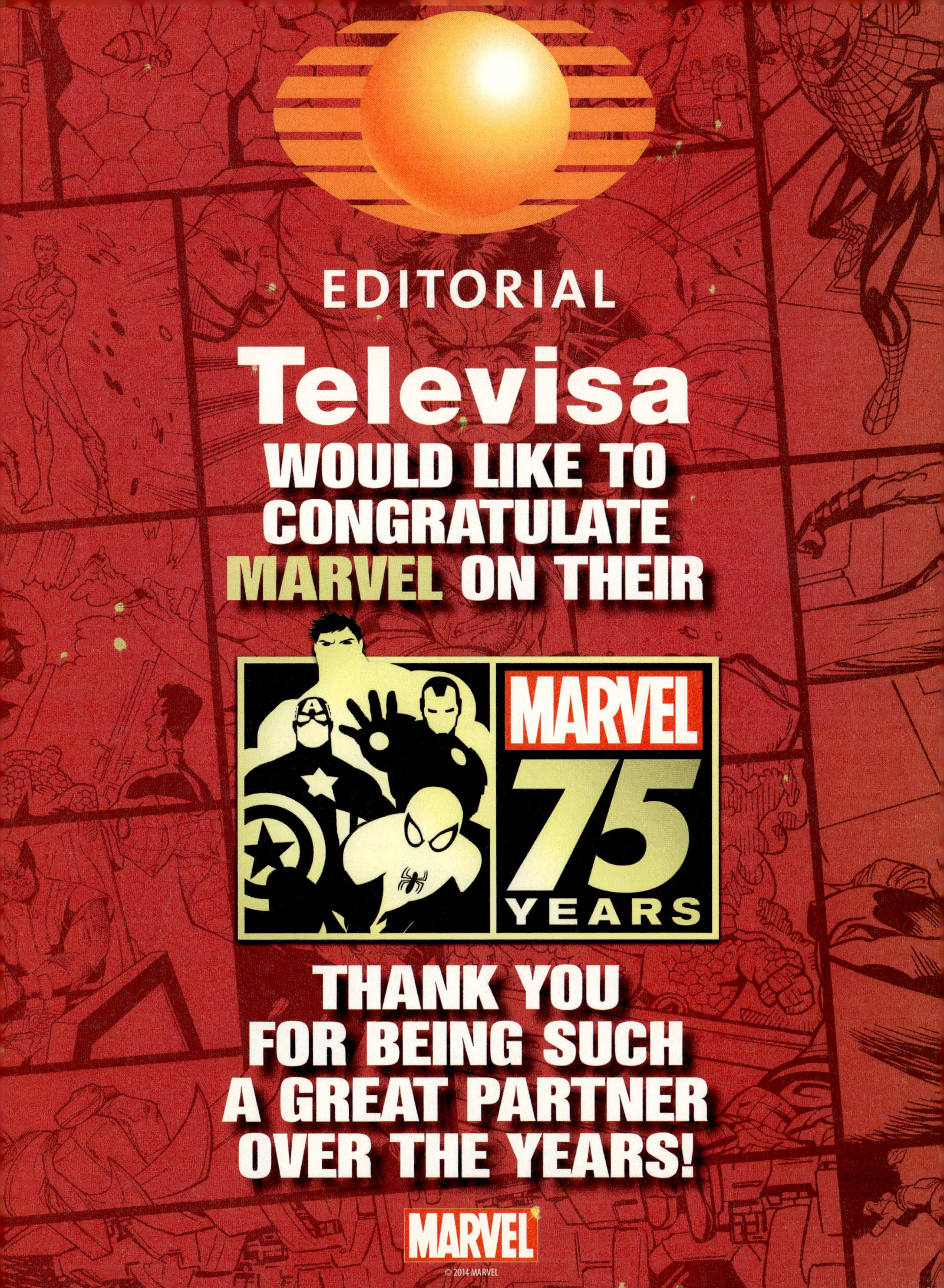

EDITORIAL
Televisa
WOULD LIKE TO
CONGRATULATE
MARVEL ON THEIR
MARVEL
75
YEARS
THANK YOU
FOR BEING SUCH
A GREAT PARTNER
OVER THE YEARS!
MARVEL
© 2014 MARVEL

It seems to me that *Amazing Spider-Man #1-100* is like one big novel of sorts. *Fantastic Four #1-100* is a novel…
I never thought of that.

They're grand stories, even though they're not prose. And in Spider-Man, you helped create an icon that resonates throughout all forms of literature, pop culture and art. Everyone from comics fans to high-minded critics have responded to Peter Parker, have reflected on his rich legacy as a fictional character. Do you consider that your great contribution to the world of writing?
I never think of it that way. I just figure I'm the luckiest guy in the world—that I wrote something that for some reason people seem to enjoy and remember, and it's still around. As I've said so many times in so many interviews, all I was thinking of at the time I wrote was just, "I hope the books sell." That way, I wouldn't be fired, and I'd be able to pay the rent. And it never occurred to me—or to anybody else at the time, I think—that people would collect them and talk about them, make movies of them… maybe I woulda paid more attention if I'd thought of that. *(Laughter.)*

Well, I hope perhaps your memory can handle this question, because it's kind of specific. There was a period of several months between when *Amazing Fantasy #15* came out, featuring Spider-Man's first appearance, and when *Amazing Spider-Man #1* hit store shelves. I know you had to wait a couple months for the sales figures proving you had a hit on your hands with Spider-Man, but there was still a several-month gap even beyond that. Was that because you were taking a lot of care to finesse this book before you launched it? Was there any reason that took a little longer than maybe it should have?
No—I don't remember. It could have been something as simple as my publisher, Martin Goodman, not being able to put it on the schedule because we didn't have a printer. You know, we had to wait 'til the printer had time for another book.

And I remember you were limited in the number of titles you could put out at that time, so you probably had to wait until a book was cancelled to clear space on the schedule.
Yeah. Yeah, could have been that, or it could have been that Steve Ditko wasn't able to start it right away—could've been anything. But as far as trying to refine the character before we launched him—I must tell you, it's a terrible thing to say—I never put any extra effort into anything. In other words, I never thought, "Boy, this is a more important book, so I'd better spend more time on it." I put as much effort as I could into everything I wrote, but I never took longer because I thought it was important.

Not even the Silver Surfer?
No, I wrote that in the same amount of time. 'Cause the one lucky thing about me, I've always been a fast writer—and since I was always my own editor, I always loved what I wrote! *(Laughter.)* "Gee, that's great! Now I'll do the next page!"

"A masterpiece!"
That's why they went quickly, 'cause I loved what I wrote—I didn't make any changes!

Did you feel like *Amazing Spider-Man #1* was going to fulfill the promise that was borne out of the response to *Amazing Fantasy #15*?
I hoped it would. But I felt that way about everything!

You did?
I felt that way about the Fantastic Four, the X-Men, the Hulk—everything I did, I liked it. And I liked the artist. Mostly it was Kirby and Ditko—then later on it was Romita, Buscema, all the guys. I liked what they did, I liked the way the pages looked when I got them back, and I always said, "Boy, this oughta do well." The only one I wasn't sure of was *Sgt. Fury*—because that was a war book, and who the hell knew with a war book? But I liked it, and I figured we would take a chance.

***Marvel Masterworks: Sgt. Fury and His Howling Commandos* includes the first 13 issues by you and Jack Kirby, and it's wonderful!**
I loved it. You know what I liked the best about it? In the Army, you talk dirty. All the soldiers talk dirty. I mean, if a four-letter

SPIDER-MAN MEETS DAREDEVIL: Two of Stan's earliest creations mix it up in the pages of *Daredevil #16*, drawn by John Romita Sr.! Jazzy John didn't know it, but this was his audition to take over *Amazing Spider-Man* from Steve Ditko!

The *Elks* Drug Awareness Program wishes to congratulate Marvel on their 75th Anniversary. We are proud to be a partner for the past 9 years, producing custom comics that are distributed into schools, helping children make healthy choices and understand drug abuse & violence.

Visit us at:

www.elkskidszone.org

The Mission of the *Elks* Drug Awareness Program is to promote constructive and cooperative approaches to the prevention of use of illicit substances by the youth of the United States of America. This is accomplished through education of students and their parents and by assisting scholastic institutions with a variety of programs and materials.

word isn't in every sentence, then you're a Nazi spy, you're not a soldier. In writing *Sgt. Fury*, I think I managed to make those guys sound like they really were in the Army, to make Fury sound like a tough sergeant, and I didn't use one dirty word! And I think that was one of my greatest achievements! *(Laughter.)*

Nick Fury is one of your characters that has a very established way of speaking—a gutsy, crusty Brooklyn guy who doesn't mince words. Lots of writers have had to follow in your footsteps to put that across.

The funny thing is, I'm not crazy about war stories, so I don't remember how many issues we did. But at one point I said, "Let's drop the book." And we got so many letters from readers wanting it back! And I didn't want to do any new ones, so we did reprints. We re-did them, and they sold about as well as the original ones!

Marvel has reprinted your original proposal for *Fantastic Four #1* in the first *Fantastic Four Omnibus*. A lot of people consider the Marvel style of storytelling to be synonymous with the advent of Marvel's super-hero comics—but did it predate those, with the Western comics you were doing? The reason I ask is that particularly with the *Rawhide Kid*—which predated *Fantastic Four* by a good year and a half—it seems you can see the gears turning a little bit on some of the puzzle pieces that would come together with the super-hero comics. You can trace certain developments back to the Westerns and even monster comics. Like the similarity of Johnny Bart, aka the Rawhide Kid, and Peter Parker, who would come a few years later.

Good. I really don't remember now what the Rawhide Kid's angle was. It's funny—my publisher, Martin, he loved the word "Kid." I mean all I had to do was come up with a title with the word "Kid" in it. You know, we had the Rawhide Kid, the Texas Kid, Kid Colt—I think we had a few others. He was big on the word "Kid."

See, I had to get all the titles okayed by Martin when I'd come up with a title.

Tell us a little bit about Martin and what he meant to you as a mentor.

Martin was not a dumb guy. He was a brilliant man, and he was good at what he did. The one thing he was great at, and taught me a lot about, was covers. See, in those days, you sold the book according to the cover mostly. Because when we started there wasn't that brand loyalty, there weren't kids saying every month, "Oh man, I can't wait for the next *Amazing Spider-Man*." They bought 'em arbitrarily. They walked to a newsstand and bought whatever cover grabbed their eye. So Martin used to teach me the best colors to put on the covers—some colors stand out better than others—and always to put the title in a splash and make a title that was provocative, and...he really taught me a lot. I became the best damned cover guy in the business, and it was because of Martin. And our books sold because of those covers!

'Course, later on we could have had a blank cover—a kid would just say, "Has the latest *Hulk* come out?" But in those days, if the cover didn't catch your eye, you wouldn't buy the book. And he was great at that.

"But in those days, if the cover didn't catch your eye you wouldn't buy the book. And he [Martin Goodman] was great at that."

Stan, are there any Steve Ditko anecdotes you haven't told yet? Because he's a big mystery in Marvel history.

Yeah, a big mystery to me!

Steve is best known for his work on *Amazing Spider-Man* and *Dr. Strange*, and was a prolific contributor to the Atlas Era monster comics. What was he like to work with?

Couldn't have been greater. I loved him. He was the best guy to work with you could ever find. Talented, dependable—in an emergency, he could bat it out fast, and it was still good. If I needed him to pencil something for somebody else, or to quickly ink something somebody had penciled 'cause the inker didn't show up...whatever it was, he was there! And he always did it beautifully, always on time, never complained. And at some point, years later, he got mad at me and he quit. And I said to him once, "What the hell did you quit for?" And he said, "*You* know!" And I don't know, and he never told me, and that was it.

Do you ever talk to him anymore?

I met him at the offices of Marvel a few years ago—or maybe it was like ten years ago, now—in New York. And he was very friendly, we talked for a while, we even talked about maybe doing a strip together.

I think you were thinking of having him as the artist for *Ravage 2099*, right?

I don't know. I don't know whether this was before or after that. I don't remember what we discussed, but the one thing he said he would never do was *Dr. Strange* or *Spider-Man*.

For a guy who's achieved so much as a comics writer and publisher, I was surprised to learn you never graduated from college.

No. I went to City College of New York at night for six months. I went there because there was a girl I met that I liked, and—I can't remember, I think I worked in the daytime, and the only way I could see her was at night. But she was going to college at night, so I figured, "Screw it, I'll go to college!" So I went there at night, and we were able to get together, 'cause she was in college. But then we broke up, so I quit City College after the six months.

THE INCREDIBLE CHANGING HULK: Stan and his creative partners had some trouble getting the Hulk out of the gate with a distinctive look and characterization. In the first panel from issue #1 (left), the Hulk is gray! The next issue, his skin color turns green (center). And in issue #4 (right), the Hulk goes from smart to dumb! Even back in those days, there were continuity concerns that could keep creators up at night!

Do you ever feel any regret about that?
Oh, I wish I had gone. There are so many things I don't know, so many things about literature, art—there are writers I've never read and so forth. So yeah, I wish I had gone to college. I always hoped I would, but then World War II broke out.

Would you have studied literature?
Oh, sure. Sure. Believe it or not, I might have wanted to also study science. I am an idiot when it comes to science, but I'm fascinated by it. I mean, I always feel guilty—even when people interview me, I feel you should be interviewing guys who are doing medical research, who are building bridges, who are—I mean, those are the people that really are doing things that count, you know? I think I'd have loved to have been a researcher. I'd have loved to have worked in a laboratory and looked for a cure for cancer. I feel those things can't be that hard to do if you just know what you're doing. But I always felt, as a matter of fact, I could solve the secret of the world. You know, everybody wonders what's it all about—where did we come from, why are we here, who is God and all of that. I always felt if I could get on top of a mountain, quietly, for two weeks, with no phone calls and nobody bothering me, I could figure it all out. But I never had the two weeks...

You've always seemed to have a "can-do" personality, a confidence that says, "I can handle this."
Yeah, things can be handled, more or less…

"Anything you throw at me, I'll give my best, and— "
(Interrupts.) Except in two areas. I cannot sing, and it kills me. My wife is the greatest singer in the world—I can't carry a tune! When I was a kid in school, they had something called the Listeners' Room, where if you couldn't carry a tune you had to sit in the Listeners' Room. I was there for my whole school career. As a kid, if I'd open my mouth once, I'd throw the whole class off-key. It was embarrassing. And I can't play a musical instrument. I can pick out a tune on a piano with one finger, but I can't play a musical instrument.

Didn't you used to have the ocarina? You used to irritate the Timely office…
(Excited. Leaps up and leans across table.) I had an ocarina, yes!

And you used to irritate Simon and Kirby with it!
Yes! Yes! They hated it!

"Who is this kid playing the ocarina?"
Everybody hated my playing! And I don't blame them. *(Laughter.)*

Did you have any particular tunes you pecked out on that?
Yeah, I could play anything—badly! *(Laughter.)* It's funny, though.

We know that you succeeded, beyond your wildest dreams, but what would Stan Lee have been when he grew up if his career in comics hadn't panned out? You could have gotten into real estate, used cars …
Oh, I love real estate, and I love cars! I always said I'd love to have been a used car salesman.

Advertising, too …
Advertising I love. When I read a magazine—you know, a slick magazine—I look at the ads before anything. If I read *Newsweek*, which I love, the ads are what I read first.

You would have been great in advertising—obviously what you learned about comic covers completely correlates to advertising.
Well, I treated all of Marvel as a big ad campaign—with the slogans "Make Mine Marvel," "Excelsior," "Hang Loose, Face Front," "'Nuff Said," little catchwords. "Welcome to the Marvel Age of Comics," all that sort of thing. I didn't think it out like a campaign, but it all was part of a big ad thing to give the company the right image, to reach the reader and have the reader feel a little excitement. It was the same with the club, the M.M.M.S. [Merry Marvel Marching Society]. I loved that; Martin made me stop that after a while, 'cause he told me we were spending too much time on it. We should have kept it. Anyway…

That kind of approach was important after the '50s witch hunts kinda scared people away from comics. You pulled back some people.
Yeah. Tried to.

Because you were saying, "Okay, it's a kid-friendly universe, your kids can come. It's fun!"
You guys know more about the things I've done than I do. I oughtta be interviewing you!

We'd love to take you up on that, Stan, but interviewing us would be nowhere near as fun, exciting, interesting and informative as interviewing you! We'd like to thank Stan for taking the time to engage in a little reverie about the subject we all love: Marvel Comics!

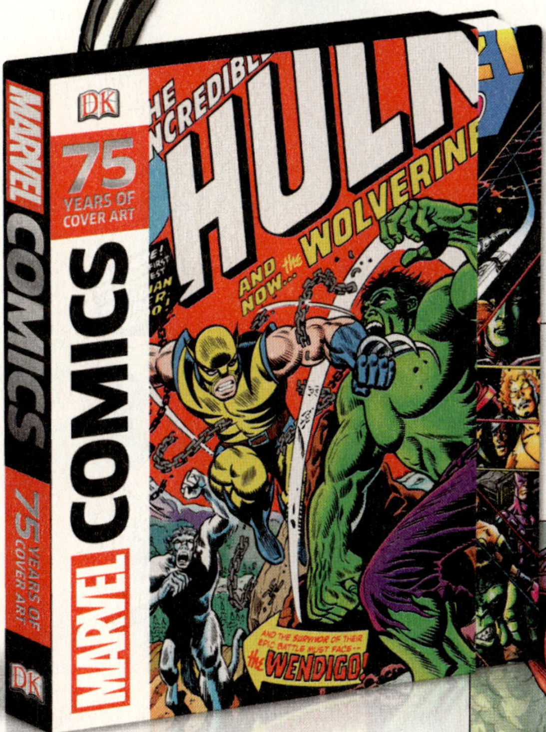

WALTER SIMONSON

AN INTERVIEW WITH A VISIONARY

BY JOHN RHETT THOMAS

THE MARVEL AGE was entering its second decade when Walter Simonson began illustrating comics for a living. After a four-year run at DC, where he drew his seminal Manhunter serial in *Detective Comics*, Simonson made his way to Marvel. By 1983, he was delivering one of the all-time classic runs of *Thor*. His first stay at Marvel spanned the '70s through the early '90s, and he recently returned to draw arcs of *Avengers* and *Indestructible Hulk*—and, thank the gods, a series of covers for *The Mighty Thor*. During this celebration of 75 years of great comic-book storytelling, we figured there was nobody better than Walter Simonson to give us a look into the life of a writer and artist who knows Marvel from so many different angles.

How did you view Marvel when you first broke into comics professionally during the early '70s?
When I came to New York in 1972 out of art school, to me Marvel was not doing the best comics that were coming out. They were good comics, but I was a big Marvel fan in the '60s—Jack Kirby, Stan Lee, Steve Ditko, Don Heck, all those guys. I read all their stuff, loved it, but by the early '70s it seemed to me that Marvel was kind of in a holding pattern while DC was trying a bunch of oddball, different things—like *Enemy Ace* and *Angel and the Ape* and all sorts of things—many of which didn't go very far or last very long, but they were still very interesting. So when I first came to New York, I first looked to DC as a place to work.

What was the scene like back then?
Comics was really a small business, and if you wanted to do comics professionally—whether writing or drawing—you pretty much had to live in New York. Now, some of the established guys like John Buscema, John Severin, guys like that, they could live somewhere else and mail things in, but of course this is before the Internet, before Federal Express—the dark ages. So you had to live in New York. I lived in Brooklyn, I lived in Queens, I eventually lived in Manhattan, and a lot of my friends did the same. I got to know a few of the guys working at Marvel.

Your very first Marvel work was a few spot illustrations for a horror magazine. Not a hugely auspicious debut!
Yeah, it was a little black-and-white horror pulp called *Haunt of Horror*. I ended up doing seven or eight different drawings for the magazine: short little squibs, chapter ends, featuring a skull lying on its side or the like.

That gave you a foot in the door with the company, but you didn't do much more with them at the time.
I did those drawings, but otherwise I didn't know the guys at Marvel all that well, so I stayed working at DC for about four years as a freelancer. I remember the first regular feature I did for Marvel, somewhere around 1976, was *Rampaging Hulk*, a black-and-white magazine

OPPOSITE PAGE:
Cover to *Thor #337* by Walter Simonson.

Marvel was launching at the time. I did the layouts for the first three issues; Doug Moench wrote the stories, Alfredo Alcala did the finishes on them. Hulk was the first mainstream Marvel character that I drew. So I got into Marvel kind of slowly—horror illustrations, then Conan stuff, then the Hulk. I wasn't starving or anything, but I kind of gradually slid in the door sideways.

You took on your first monthly comic at Marvel in June 1977. That was the first issue of *Thor* you drew. Did Thor have any special significance to you at the time?

I was always a big Thor fan. I was reading comics at the time when Marvel had only about 11 titles. Remember those days? *(Laughter.)*

SIMONSON ON THE RAMPAGE: Simonson's first sequential art for Marvel was in the Hulk's 1977 black-and-white magazine. (Art from *Rampaging Hulk #2.*)

I don't remember them, but I'm aware of them!

Comics sold for 20 cents or whatever. I bought all the Marvels—Thor was really my ultimate favorite. I was familiar with Norse mythology before I discovered Marvel Comics. I had read Norse myths as a child—my parents had a book of them in the house. Loved the stories, and I was thrilled the first time I found a Marvel comic that starred Thor. I had never seen a Marvel comic at that time. The comic started out with this big fight where Thor and Odin and the warriors of Asgard are all sailing off in a flying Viking ship, going off to fight the Frost Giants or whatever bad guy it was. And there's a little note at the bottom that said, "We promised old Jack Kirby we'd let him open up with a bang, so here it is!"—or something like that—signed "Stan."

At the time I read it I had no idea who Jack Kirby was. The way it was phrased, I thought, "Wow, some fan must have written in and said, 'Gee, I'd love to see a big fight with these guys!'" *(Laughter.)* But I remember reading the comic and being wowed by it. It was this rough-hewn, energetic, vital story. And fun! That's what really captured my imagination.

So you were a Thor lover.

I was. When Len Wein was writer/editor, he offered me a shot at drawing it. I did layouts instead of full pencils.

We did very much a classic Thor, which was a lot of what Marvel was about at the time. Not everything was like that: I think *Master of Kung Fu* felt like nothing else. Starlin had done *Captain Marvel* and *Warlock*, and those were different. But with *Thor*, Len and I felt like we were doing a classic take on the stories and characters. Tony DeZuniga did most of the finishes. I got inked by Joe Sinnott on an issue or two. I'm not sure Joe knew what to make of my layouts! *(Laughter.)* It was still kinda early days for me.

Who was your influence at that time of your career?

I'm a big Jack Kirby fan from the get-go, so a lot of my work has Kirby underpinnings. But when I got into comics professionally I began to have some access to work I had never seen. In particular I saw European work: Moebius, Jim Holdaway's *Modesty Blaise*, Jean-Claude M zi res' *Val rian: Agent of Space and Time.* Palacios out of Spain was doing an El Cid comic I liked; they were sort of cartoony but very well-rendered, very design-oriented. I began bringing a lot of that work into my own stuff. Maybe a little less in my first run on *Thor*, where it really was a Marvel comic—in the best sense of that at the time.

After that you left super heroes for sci-fi: a *Close Encounters* adaptation, the Heavy Metal graphic novel of *Alien*, a run on *Battlestar Galactica*—and you did *Star Wars*.

When I first got into the business, science fiction was only a small part of the comics industry. It was mostly about super heroes. *Star Wars* changed that. I like to think that for a little while, at least by the end of the '70s through the early '80s, I was doing every science-fiction comic they were putting out. *(Laughter.)*

I had been a science-fiction reader in high school all through art school and I really enjoyed sci-fi as a genre, and so doing it in comics was sort of a natural extension of my interests. And I had a chance to do *Star Wars*, *Battlestar Galactica* and *Alien*. I never did *Star Trek* as a comic. I did a cover or two so at least I got a toe in the water on that.

It was fun. I wasn't directing my career at the time: "Okay, I've done super heroes, it's time to do science fiction!" This stuff just presented itself. Serendipity.

***Battlestar Galactica* is where you started writing. That wasn't exactly one of the most popular Marvel titles at the time.**

I had written a couple little squibs in the early '70s, little one-page things that DC used to do in the war books in the early '70s—but yes, my first comic-book writing was *Galactica*.

I was drawing it at the time. Roger McKenzie had been my writer. When he left the book, Weezy [Simonson's wife, Louise] was the editor and she asked if I wanted to take a crack at writing it. And I said, "Sure!" Of course, I was nervous. (*Laughter.*)

But everybody starts somewhere! I did four out of the last five issues, and I found I really enjoyed it.

As a result of those four issues, I bumped into Archie Goodwin and he said he read them. He was very complimentary—which thrilled me, because there was nobody whose opinion I valued more than Archie's. He was a master of comics: a wonderful editor, a wonderful writer and really a master cartoonist—which is less well-known. He said there was a movie coming out and Marvel was doing an adaptation of it, and would I be interested in writing the adaptation for John Buscema to do layouts for and Klaus Janson to finish. I said, "Sure, what is it?" He said, "Something called *Raiders of the Lost Ark*." I told him ,"Sure, what the heck? I don't even know what that means, but I'm happy to do it."

So my fifth, sixth and seventh professional writing jobs were three issues of *Raiders of the Lost Ark*. It was from the full script, so it wasn't exactly like I was writing from scratch. I didn't write it cold. But that worked out very well. Once again, Archie was very complimentary about it. He had begun to push me in the writing direction. About the time that was wrapping up, Mark Gruenwald—who was the editor of *Thor* at the time—talked to me.

And now we come back to *Thor*. That's quite an interesting career you'd been putting together by that point.

When I got into comics in the early '70s—and I have had these discussions with Howard Chaykin and some other guys, as well—we all really thought comics were dying. At that time, there was no direct market, there were no comic shops—there was just newsstand sales, and the newsstand sales were diminishing. The trend was there, and we could all see it.

Now, we all loved comics. We all wanted to be in the business, but we did so thinking that after a few years—maybe five years or so—we'd all have to go out and get real jobs. That comics would really be gone as an art form and a commercial form. Those days were going to be over, but we wanted to do comics while they were still around. So we jumped in with both feet and had a fabulous time. And then in large part thanks to Phil Seuling, the direct market began to develop different business models, and comics began to recover from what we thought was going to be the long decline into oblivion.

THOR CLASSIC: **Simonson's first run on *Thor* during the '70s featured a more classic approach to the God of Thunder. (Art from *Thor #271*.)**

And suddenly we had longer jobs and longer careers than anyone ever expected to have at the time. It was such a joy to do them.

So how did you and Mark Gruenwald plan the new direction for *Thor*?

Mark called me into the office one day, and offered me a chance to write and draw Thor. I made the proviso that it was carte blanche. *Thor* wasn't selling well at the time. If the book bombed, nobody would notice. But if it worked, they'd say, "Simonson's a genius!"

I used the goofy nuttiness of the Lee/Kirby *Thor* as my inspiration, and tried to bring at least that sense of joy to my work. So I had a direction, and Mark was true to his word: He really gave me a chance to do the complete package. It was a thrill, and on a character I loved. I couldn't have asked for a better deal.

You really did throw out the rulebook in a lot of ways with *Thor*.

I never really thought about it that way. I was just telling stories. There were some nutty, crazed layouts—but largely what I tried to do was to let the art and the storytelling and the layouts in particular come out of the story I'm trying to tell. In the case of *Thor*, to me it was an odd but interesting mix of saga-inspired stories and science fiction: The epic fantasy story looked back to the past, the science fiction looked to the future. And I thought that gave *Thor* an interesting tension in a way between the old and the new that I didn't see in any other books.

One element of your *Thor* run was a remodeling of Asgard.

That's the one thing that I can tip my hat to. Jack always drew an Asgard that was very science-fictiony: big towers, swooping slides, platforms, statuary and all sorts of stuff. But when I had the chance to draw Asgard, I took the chance to go back and reconsider all the visuals. I didn't write a story that explained why this was all so different—I didn't think it was important. At least it wasn't then—maybe continuity fanatics would be nuts now if you did the same thing. But I based my versions of Asgard off the stave churches of Northern Europe and Scandinavia, which is kind of ironic I suppose for a group of Viking gods.

There aren't any surviving Viking buildings, but the stave churches were done not long after the Viking era; they have old dragon heads on the rooflines, things of that sort.

DCBS CONGRATULATES MARVEL ON 75 YEARS OF STORY TELLING

DCBS

FROM ALL YOUR FRIENDS AT

DISCOUNT COMIC BOOK SERVICE

WWW.DCBSERVICE.COM

And I took that as my model and built on it in a very different way—with a much rougher, wooden and hopefully more Nordic feel to it. I didn't make a big deal out of it. I just went ahead and did it.

I remember *Thor* came out when I was 12 or 13. It really stood out. It also sold a ton.
(*Laughter.*) Well, I'm glad. There's a lid for every pot. The book did well. I went over to Supersnipe, which was a comic shop that used to exist on the Upper East Side. A couple days after the book came out, I thought I'd go over there to buy a couple of copies, just for my files. I went over, and they said they were sold out. I said, "I'm sorry?" They said, "Well, we're sold out." I said, "We're talking about *Thor #337*?"

"Oh yeah, they're all gone, and we can't get any more." At first I thought, "Wow, that's really cool! How about that?" But then I thought, well crap, how am I going to get a couple copies for my files? (*Laughter.*) I had no expectation. Nobody really did.

I missed getting that issue, and there was no way I could afford getting a back issue at that time.
It's much cheaper now! (*Laughter.*)

One guy who really stood out on that book besides you was John Workman. You let him loose on a lot of great lettering.
We had first worked together on the *Alien* graphic novel. He had been art director at *Heavy Metal* in the '70s. He was the guy who hired me to do the art on that book—but he also lettered *Alien,* and his work was a revelation to me. John was lettering things the way I would have liked to have done had I been a letterer. His sound effects, his display lettering, were really typographical and calligraphic forms—which is what I really liked and had done myself. In my earliest work, I had done a lot of my own display lettering. It's part of your composition; it's part of the visual appeal of your work. It's really important, and it's often overlooked.

By the time I was doing *Thor*, John was no longer at *Heavy Metal.* His little letter forms were quite lovely, so I totally grabbed him and got him on that book. And pretty much almost everything I've done since those days, John has been lettering for me.

His work brings a very distinctive and very rigorous look to the lettering in a book. I think John's work complements what I do in a way that I would never have thought I'd find. I never thought I'd find a letterer who would be so much a part of my stuff as I did. I was incredibly lucky, and it's something I've always been aware of.

You have done some exciting work recently on *Avengers* and *Indestructible Hulk*. What is your take on the industry now compared to the way it was when you broke in?
I don't know. It's different. I think the business models are different. They partly have moved into a reprint approach where things are done in arcs that are then collected in paperbacks and hardcovers. Back when I was doing *Thor*, even 30 years ago, you did a comic, it got published, and then it disappeared. Except for finding it as a back issue in a comic shop somewhere, you never saw it again. It very rarely was reprinted.

That was just beginning to happen when I was on *Fantastic Four*, where three issues of the series got collected into a little trade paperback at the time. And other stuff was beginning to be traded, as well. The result is that now it seems to me that a lot of stories are done as five- or six-issue story arcs. That has some pluses and some minuses, but the structure of comics has changed because of it.

MODERN MASTERWORKS: Marvel fans were treated to Simonson's return in 2012 to pencil arcs of *Avengers* and *Indestructible Hulk*, plus a series of covers for *The Mighty Thor*. (Cover to *Mighty Thor #14*.)

Now that I'm out of mainstream comics, I don't look as much as I once did. But I see a lot of really beautiful drawing in comics now. The few writers I've dealt with—Brian Michael Bendis and Mark Waid—seem to be having a great time doing what they're doing. And I would hope that is true for the younger writers and artists. I would hope that in this era they'd be able to write and draw stories that they wanted to do, and really have as much fun as I was able to. None of us got into the business back then to make a living, but the doing it was the real treat. I would hope they find the same enthusiasm and pleasure. •

Thank you, Walter! The entire '80s run of Simonson's Thor is available in a series of classic trades: *Thor by Walter Simonson Vols. 1-5*. •

EVENT HORIZON

THE CROSSOVERS THAT DEFINED THE MARVEL UNIVERSE!

By Jess Harrold & John Rhett Thomas

The only thing better than reading the adventures of your favorite hero or super team? Reading the adventures of more than one of them together! And the only thing better than that? All of them at the same time! In its seven-and-a-half-decade history, the House of Ideas has a proud record of delivering the best crossover events. This list builds a timeline of the most pivotal Marvel events from the late '80s to present, with a few seminal moments from prior years thrown in for good measure: These are the team-up tales that changed everything; the crossovers that consumed the whole darn publishing schedule; the not-a-hoax, not-a-dream, not-an-imaginary-story events that shaped the Marvel Universe as we know it!

1973

AVENGERS/DEFENDERS WAR

A clash of the titans!

By 1973, stories crossing over from one title to another were not without precedent, but never before had it been done with as much gusto as in the Avengers/Defenders War. Parlaying the fanfare surrounding the recent launch of *Defenders*, this crossover did what Marvel does best: pit its beloved characters against each other! Iron Man vs. Hawkeye! Subby vs. Cap! Surfer vs. Vision! HULK VS. THOR!!! If that ain't a book that sells itself, I'm canceling my subscription to *FOOM!*

1984

MARVEL SUPER HEROES SECRET WARS

Marvel goes to infinity and Beyonder in the official comic of the action-figure line!

Good and evil, locked in eternal conflict. But which is stronger? There's only one way to find out: FIIIIGHT!!! That's the conclusion reached by playfully curious cosmic entity the Beyonder. In the simplest — and best — premise of all time for a super-hero slobberknocker, the Beyonder toys with Marvel's heroes and villains, whisking them to Battleworld just to see who wins. Gasp as Hulk holds up a mountain! Thrill as Doom seizes the Beyonder's power! Gag as a very '80s Wasp locks lips with Magneto...

1985

SECRET WARS II

The birth of the line-wide cross-title extravaganza!

This sprawling story of the Beyonder's visit to Earth, told across a nine-issue limited series and more than 30 tie-ins, ushered in the age of the crossover mega-event. Though not universally popular, there's no doubt there is fun to be had in some of the offbeat stories that resulted. Who didn't want to see Simonson's Thor team with Power Pack? Other chapters were absolute gems, such as Matt Murdock accepting — then selflessly surrendering — the gift of sight in *Daredevil #223*. Best of all, though, there's the sheer '80s entertainment factor of the Beyonder and his Hasselhoff hair.

1988

EVOLUTIONARY WAR

Marvel's annuals evolve!

In an innovative move, eleven of Marvel's summer annuals were given over to a single story as our heroes faced the threat of the High Evolutionary and his bid to accelerate human evolution to its conclusion. It's an unfamiliar lineup of Earth's Mightiest that inevitably rides to the rescue in *Avengers Annual #11*, the concluding chapter. Jocasta assembles a team of reservists that includes Steve Rogers, known then simply as "the Captain," and the bouncing Beast, making a welcome return. Crashing the party, the previously villainous female Yellowjacket redeems herself and writes her footnote in Avengers history.

1989

INFERNO

Heroes fight fires as Manhattan burns!

While the earlier *Mutant Massacre* may have caught Thor, Daredevil and Power Pack in its wake — and the influence of *Fall of the Mutants* spread even wider — *Inferno* was the first X-centric extravaganza to cast its shadow over the whole Marvel Universe. Skies darken in a demonic transformation of Manhattan as Limbo's legions invade — and civilians, inanimate objects and X-Men alike are distorted by evil forces. As Manhattan is engulfed by flames, Cyclops comes face-to-face with the ex-wife from hell — literally! Transformed into the evil Goblin Queen, former Mrs. Summers Madelyne Pryor targets her child — the baby that would one day become Cable. *Inferno* paved the way for other '90s X-overs such as the *X-Tinction Agenda*, *X-Cutioner's Song* (spotting a theme?), *Fatal Attractions*, *Bloodties* (with bonus Avengers) and *Phalanx Covenant*.

1989

ATLANTIS ATTACKS

Out of the ocean comes the second annual spectacular!

There was something fishy going on in 1989's annuals. Deviant priest Ghaur, Lemurian queen Lyra and then-Atlantean monarch Attuma join forces to recreate the Serpent Crown and aid Elder God Set's bid to take over the world — a plan that involves some of Marvel's most prominent super heroines being recruited as Set's seven brides! Rather than holding their peace, heroes unite to stop the septuple wedding — but they'll have to face an Atlantean invasion and an infestation of serpent men first!

1989-1990

ACTS OF VENGEANCE

Heroes and villains switch partners, Do-Si-Do!

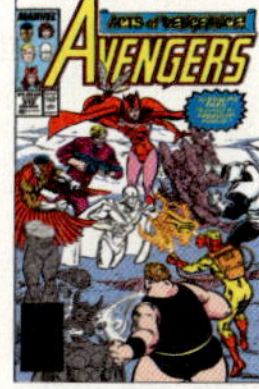

Marvel ushered in the '90s with this delightfully simple premise: A bunch of "big bads," tired of a cycle of defeat against predictable opponents, decide to change dance partners. Three months of unfamiliar match-ups ensue across the Marvel line before infighting among the evildoers wrecks the plan and the Machiavellian mastermind stands revealed. The final parting shot — a gigantic Tri-Sentinel robot unleashed on Manhattan — is casually dealt with by a conveniently cosmically powered Spider-Man. (Don't ask.)

1991

INFINITY GAUNTLET

The universe in the palm of Thanos' hand!

The first chapter of cosmic specialist Jim Starlin's Infinity series — which also includes *Infinity Crusade*, *Infinity War*, *Infinity Abyss* and the *Infinity Revelation* original graphic novel — sees lovestruck Thanos send Death the ultimate bloody Valentine: He wipes out half of all life in the universe with the titular glove, setting a pattern of strictly temporary universal destruction that has become a staple of the grand-scale super-hero crossover. You know it will all turn out okay in the end, though — we're all still here, right? But that shouldn't stop you from enjoying the ride — and the unusual sight of Marvel's greatest heroes getting brutally slain!

1995

AGE OF APOCALYPSE

Altered history leads to Apocalypse now!

When Charles Xavier's son, Legion, travels back into the past to shoot Magneto, good ol' Chuck's bravery leads him to take the bullet. The resulting paradox ushers in the dawning of the *Age of Apocalypse*. For several months, all X-books were replaced by new titles featuring fresh spins on Marvel's merry mutants — including the now-pacifist Magneto and his X-Men! Enormously successful and enduringly popular, the ideas, characters and designs on display have come to influence years of subsequent mutant mythology.

1996

ONSLAUGHT

When Xavier stumbles, heroes fall!

Perhaps Xavier should have stayed dead. When the chickens come home to roost and Xavier's mind-wipe of Magneto results in a monstrous psionic fusion of their two consciousnesses in a single entity, Marvel's heroes face Onslaught! With the powers of both, but very much Magneto's fashion sense, Onslaught at first seeks to forcibly preserve mutantkind before ultimately marking both it and humanity for destruction. Only a wide-scale heroic sacrifice can save the day, leaving life-long fans of the Avengers and Fantastic Four dumbstruck as their favorite characters seemingly die, and titles enjoyed for decades come to an end.

1996-1997

HEROES REBORN & HEROES RETURN

Marvel's heroes get a new image!

In the wake of *Onslaught*, an industry-changing initiative ushered in new issue #1s for *Captain America*, *Avengers*, *Iron Man* and *Fantastic Four*, with superstars such as Jim Lee and Rob Liefeld returning to Marvel to tell radically different tales set on a whole other world. A world in which Cap doesn't even have an "A" on his head (at least at first). This major culture shock for readers would last for just over a year until the events of *Heroes Return* would reveal the characters' true fate — and Franklin Richards' role in it — before restoring these celebrated super folks to a grateful Earth.

2004

AVENGERS DISASSEMBLED

The Avengers don't just disband — they disintegrate.

And there came a day, unlike any other, when Earth's Mightiest Heroes found themselves torn asunder by one of their own. In Bendis' cataclysmic opening act on Avengers, an insane Scarlet Witch rips the team apart, leading to the deaths of stalwart members Ant-Man, Vision and — in a literal blaze of glory — Hawkeye. In a storyline that rocked all the team members' solo titles and brought down the curtain on the main series after more than 500 issues, the old order endeth.

2004-2005

SECRET WAR

Super-spy games and shadowy shenanigans!

A number of writer Brian Michael Bendis' later New Avengers — including Captain America, Spider-Man, Wolverine and Luke Cage — join with frequent allies Black Widow and Daredevil on a covert mission orchestrated by Nick Fury to overthrow the Latverian government. The resulting reprisal — in the form of a full-scale attack on New York by then-Latverian leader Lucia von Bardas and an army of technologically upgraded super villains — sends Fury into hiding for years to come. In his place, the series introduces new S.H.I.E.L.D. Director Maria Hill, a major player in the Marvel Universe to this day.

2005

HOUSE OF M

"Everything changes" is no empty hype for Marvel's mutants.

In the wake of her mental breakdown, the Scarlet Witch rewrites reality, making many heroes' dreams come true in a bid to distract them from putting things right. The plan unravels, largely due to Wolverine's now-restored memory and a mysterious young girl named Layla who "knows stuff." The status quo is restored — with one key twist — as Wanda utters the ominous phrase, "No more mutants." Perhaps "only something like 198 mutants" might have been more accurate, but not nearly as powerful an ending.

2007

WORLD WAR HULK

Hulk smash... Earth!

Remember that saying about the madder Hulk gets, the stronger Hulk gets? Well, after being tricked into outer space by his friends, fighting his way to the throne of his violent adopted homeworld and then losing everything — including his pregnant queen — Jade Jaws is angrier than ever. Tony Stark, Reed Richards and pretty much everybody else he blames won't like it when he returns. Sorry, guys, you can't say he never warned you.

2006-2007

NEW AVENGERS: ILLUMINATI

The ruling class you never knew existed!

Iron Man. Dr. Strange. Charles Xavier. Reed Richards. Black Bolt. Namor. Kings and leaders of men, protecting an Earth that never asked them to, in a covert crossover stretching back decades! First seen together in *New Avengers #7*,

the members of the Illuminati actually joined forces in the aftermath of the Kree-Skrull War and met regularly until they were split by the tensions of the Civil War's impending superhuman Registration Act — though the events of *Avengers vs. X-Men* would bring (most of) the band back together. *New Avengers: Illuminati* shone a light on the secret history of the Marvel Universe — and the fateful decisions made by this shadowy group.

2007-2008

MESSIAH COMPLEX

A new Hope!

Since the Decimation wrought by the Scarlet Witch, mutantkind had been perched perilously on the precipice of extinction, with little chance of revival. That all changed with the birth of a single child — the first mutant born since what had come to be known as M-Day. As the X-Men race to beat a range of deadly threats to the girl, shocking sacrifices are made and allegiances are shattered. Beginning the saga of the girl who will be known as Hope Summers, *Messiah CompleX* set the course for years of storytelling across *Messiah War*, *Schism* and *Avengers vs. X-Men*, and re-established the mutant crossover tradition that continues with events like *Battle of the Atom*.

2006

CIVIL WAR

Iron Man vs. Cap in a battle for the ages!

Whose side were you on? Chances are, the one that lost. Marvel's super heroes are put through the wringer by writer Mark Millar and artist Steve McNiven as their community takes the blame for a devastating tragedy. Tony Stark and

Reed Richards' great Initiative — registration and training for superhumans — splits teams and families down the middle as Cap's band of civil libertarians defies his best friend, Iron Man. Lots of stories claim "the universe will never be the same." With repercussions that reverberate to this day, this one delivered.

2006-2007

ANNIHILATION & ANNIHILATION CONQUEST

Marvel cosmic shoots for the stars!

Earth takes a back seat in these outer-space extravaganzas — in which the galaxy is laid to waste first by Annihilus' insectoid horde, and then by the techno-organic Phalanx. But two Terran warriors, Nova and Star-Lord, stand proudly on the front lines as two devastating wars reshape the cosmos. While many heroes fall, others are reborn as the long-neglected cosmic corner of the Marvel Universe returns to prominence — with series *War of Kings*, *Realm of Kings* and *The Thanos Imperative* following in the wake of these events. Perhaps the gloom of *Annihilation* was needed to help the stars shine that much brighter.

2008

SECRET INVASION

Who do you trust?

Earth's heroes are ravaged by infighting from the events of *Civil War* and *World War Hulk*. The universe's guardians are distracted by the *Annihilation* events. What better time for the Skrulls to exact revenge on their Terran enemies and take the planet for their own? Years worth of delicately sown seeds bear fruit as alien impostors stand revealed, and bereft Spider-Woman fans realize all their beloved character's high-profile appearances in recent years were the Skrull Queen in disguise. As the reunited heroes rally, it is an opportunistic Norman Osborn who strikes the killing blow to the Skrull plot, ushering in his own Dark Reign.

2009

DARK REIGN

Osborn in the U.S.A. as Norman takes control!

With Tony Stark and S.H.I.E.L.D. discredited as a result of *Secret Invasion*, new flavor-of-the-month Norman Osborn is handed the keys to the kingdom as head of replacement peacekeeping force H.A.M.M.E.R. As comic covers proclaim his Dark Reign, Osborn keeps a secret cabal of villains lurking in the shadows while he assembles his own public team of Avengers — all while constantly struggling to hold his sociopathic team, and his own mental stability, in check.

2010

SIEGE

The Asgard-Midgard War!

Under the subtle manipulations of Loki, Norman Osborn engineers a tragic incident that justifies a full-scale assault on Asgard, which is hovering over U.S. soil. As the Siege turns into a full-scale superhuman war between Osborn's forces and the Avengers, Asgard falls, Osborn's villainy is revealed to the world, and the awesome threat of the Void is unleashed. After years of turmoil, the Avengers have a chance to usher in a new Heroic Age — but a high price must be paid to get there.

2010

SHADOWLAND

Daredevil becomes the man without friends!

Just as *Annihilation* put Marvel's cosmic cast back on the intergalactic map, *Shadowland* shone a light on the heroes of New York's dark and dangerous back alleys. But for the street-level super-types, the threat comes from one of their own. Having sought to bend his mortal enemies to his will as the new leader of the Hand, Daredevil lets his halo slip under their malignant influence. The Man Without Fear succumbs to hate, and that leads him to the dark side. A cadre of urban warriors as diverse as Spider-Man, Luke Cage, Ghost Rider and the Shroud unite in a battle to save Matt Murdock's soul.

2011

FEAR ITSELF

There is nothing to fear except the Serpent!

A forgotten evil as old as time returns — courtesy of Sin, the Red Skull's daughter. The Serpent — banished from Asgard by his brother, Odin — returns to drop the hammer on Midgard. All seven hammers in fact, each in the hand of one of the world's most powerful superhumans — including Juggernaut, the Thing and the Hulk — possessed as the Serpent's Worthy! As battle rages across the Marvel line, Captain America, Thor and Iron Man stand proud against the Serpent's nasties and Sin's Nazis — and one will make the ultimate sacrifice.

2012

AVENGERS VS. X-MEN

Earth's Mightiest Heroes vs. the Children of the Atom!

When the deadly Phoenix returns to Earth, the Avengers are unwilling to leave the fight to the X-Men. To Captain America, the Phoenix threatens destruction — but to Cyclops, it offers the hope of salvation for his people, who have already been torn apart by *Schism*. Marvel's two greatest leaders wage war — with the Phoenix's intended host, Hope Summers, trapped in the middle. Before peace is declared, a great loss will be suffered, and the future of mutantkind will be rewritten.

2013

AGE OF ULTRON

Brian Michael Bendis destroys the Marvel Universe!

The series begins with Ultron triumphant, the world nigh-ended and what few heroes remain faced with a stark choice: submit or perish. But such desperate times call for desperate measures, and Wolverine is prepared to take them. Believing the world will be a better place without Ultron's creator, Hank Pym, Logan heads back in time to achieve exactly that. But will the new present he creates be any better than the one he left behind? The battle is on to save history and yet somehow defeat Ultron — and the collateral damage may well be the very boundaries of reality themselves! Chaos results across the Marvel Multiverse — not least when the avenging angel Angela makes her dramatic entrance!

2013

INFINITY

Thanos' invasion plunges Earth into Inhumanity!

Redefining the word "epic" as it applies to comic-book events, *Infinity* saw Earth threatened with not one, not two, but three extinction-level threats. With the Avengers in space heading off the ancient race of Builders that have marked the planet for destruction, the Mad Titan Thanos (c'mon, the name of the series gave it away, right?) seizes his moment to strike, in search of his last remaining offspring. But the Illuminati already have their own reality-threatening issues to contend with — and one among them, Black Bolt, reacts with a world-changing Hail Mary. The transformative effects of his terrifying Terrigen Bomb bring about the new age of Inhumanity.

2014

ORIGINAL SIN

Who dispatches the Watcher?

The unthinkable happens when the Watcher is murdered on the moon. With Uatu dead, the question switches from "What If?" to "Whodunnit?" as Nick Fury — the *original* Nick Fury — takes point as lead investigator and assembles a remarkable roster of heroes to play detective, each with their own very particular set of skills. But Uatu was not simply the victim of homicide. Somebody took his eyes, the repository of all he witnessed. As secret after secret is revealed and stones begin to be cast, is there anyone out there who is without sin?

MEET MARVEL'S 2014 YOUNG GUNS

No comic-book publisher *has boasted better, more diverse artistic talent during the last 75 years than Marvel. Every few years, a new crop of skilled young artists steps to the fore with a fresh way of looking at the House of Ideas and its characters. For the last eight years, Marvel has regularly spotlighted the cream of the crop as its Young Guns; previous classes have included heavyweights like Jim Cheung, Olivier Coipel, Steve McNiven, Leinil Yu, Marko Djurdjevic, Daniel Acuna and more.*

When your roster includes that level of talent, it's worth bragging about. "I think it underscores our reputation as a publisher who is always on the lookout for new talent, and cements the fact that we do not have a house style here at Marvel," Editor in Chief Axel Alonso says of the Young Guns initiative. "Great artists come in all forms. Each of these artists is very different from the next." To celebrate Marvel's wonderful history of 75 years of groundbreaking art, we present this gallery of art by 2014's Young Guns: Mahmud Asrar, Nick Bradshaw, David Marquez, Sara Pichelli, Valerio Schiti and Ryan Stegman.

MAHMUD ASRAR

FROM:
Ankara, Turkey;
half-Austrian, half-Pakistani

FAVORITE CHARACTER TO DRAW:
Storm

TITLE/CHARACTER YOU'D LOVE TO DRAW:
Uncanny X-Men or All-New X-Men

ARTISTIC INSPIRATION:
Life and things I find beautiful

FAVORITE ARTIST PEER:
Olivier Coipel

CHECKLIST:
Avengers: The Initiative, Nova, She-Hulk: Cosmic Collision, Siege: Young Avengers, Shadowland: Power Man, Thunderbolts, War Machine, War of Kings: Warriors, Wolverine & the X-Men

Cover to *Indestructible Hulk Annual #1*, layout (inset) and pencils.

Hulk sketch.

Cover to *Wolverine & the X-Men (2014) #1*, pencils and inks.

NICK BRADSHAW

FROM:
Moncton, New Brunswick, Canada

FAVORITE CHARACTER TO DRAW:
Hulk

TITLE/CHARACTER YOU'D LOVE TO DRAW:
Hulk, Fantastic Four, Spider-Man, Marvel Monsters

ARTISTIC INSPIRATION:
Arthur Adams, Mike Wieringo

FAVORITE ARTIST PEER:
Arthur Adams

CHECKLIST:
Astonishing X-Men, Guardians of the Galaxy, Inhumanity, Uncanny X-Men Annual, Wolverine & the X-Men

Cover to *Guardians of the Galaxy (2013) #15*, pencils and inks.

Variant cover to *Amazing Spider-Man (2014) #1*, pencils and inks.

Cover to *Inhumanity #2*, pencils and inks.

Cover to *Guardians of the Galaxy (2013) #14*, pencils and inks.

Cover to *Wolverine & the X-Men #33*, pencils and inks, with rough design layouts.

Book Inhumans Issue cover Story Page # Artist(s) Nick Bradshaw.

Variant cover to *Inhumanity #1*, pencils and inks.

DAVID MARQUEZ

FROM:
Born in London, England; raised in Houston, Texas

FAVORITE CHARACTER TO DRAW:
Miles Morales

TITLE/CHARACTER YOU'D LOVE TO DRAW:
X-Men

ARTISTIC INSPIRATION:
Travis Charest, Jorge Zaffino, Bill Sienkiewicz, Jim Lee

FAVORITE ARTIST PEER:
Jamie McKelvie

CHECKLIST:
All-New X-Men, Cataclysm: Ultimate Spider-Man, Fantastic Four: Season One, Guardians of the Galaxy, Miles Morales: The Ultimate Spider-Man, Secret Warriors, Ultimate Comics Spider-Man

Variant cover to *Legendary Star-Lord #1*, pencils and inks.

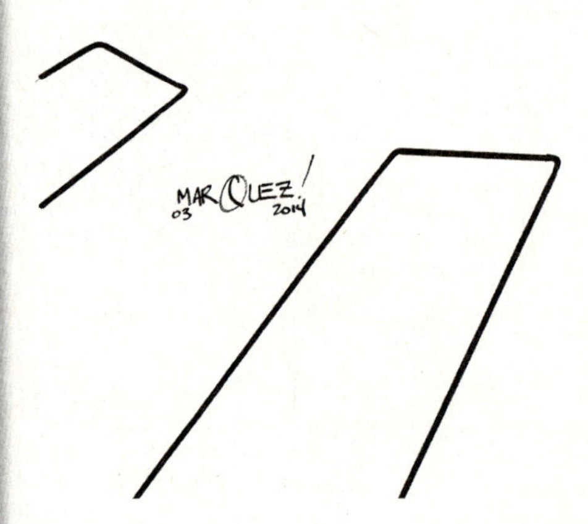

Rogue from the cover to *Young Guns 2014 Sampler #1*, pencils and inks.

Cover to *Miles Morales: The Ultimate Spider-Man #4*, pencils and inks.

Cover to *Miles Morales: The Ultimate Spider-Man #1*, pencils and inks.

Cover to *Miles Morales: The Ultimate Spider-Man #2*, pencils and inks.

SARA PICHELLI

FROM:
Rome, Italy

FAVORITE CHARACTER TO DRAW:
Storm

TITLE/CHARACTER YOU'D LOVE TO DRAW:
X-Men

ARTISTIC INSPIRATION:
Gustav Klimt, Claire Wendling, Egon Schiele, Sergio Toppi, Alberto Breccia

FAVORITE ARTIST PEER:
Stuart Immonen, Jason Pearson

CHECKLIST:
Eternals, Girl Comics, Guardians of the Galaxy, Namora, NYX: No Way Home, Runaways, Spider-Men, Ultimate Comics Spider-Man, Ultimate Spider-Man, X-Men: Pixie Strikes Back

Venom from *Ultimate Comics Spider-Man (2011) #20*, pencils and inks.

Miles Morales from *Ultimate Comics Spider-Man (2011) #2*, pencils and inks.

Groot from *Guardians of the Galaxy (2013) #4*, pencils and inks.

Angela from *Guardians of the Galaxy (2013) #5*, pencils and inks.

Gamora from *Guardians of the Galaxy (2013) #4*, pencils and inks.

Book Mighty Avengers Issue# 06 Page# 18 ARTIST schiti

VALERIO SCHITI

FROM:
Rome, Italy

FAVORITE CHARACTER TO DRAW:
Every time I take a new book, I fall in love with a new character: Sif, Beta Ray Bill, Hank Pym, White Tiger, Dr. Strange

TITLE/CHARACTER YOU'D LOVE TO DRAW:
Gambit

ARTISTIC INSPIRATION:
Stuart Immonen

FAVORITE ARTIST PEER:
Chris Samnee

CHECKLIST:
Avengers A.I., Ghost Rider, Guardians of the Galaxy, Journey Into Mystery, Mighty Avengers, New Avengers

Falcon from *Mighty Avengers (2013) #6*, layout (inset), and pencils and inks.

CONGRATULATIONS
MARVEL
ON YOUR 75TH ANNIVERSARY!
RUBIE'S
FROM YOUR FRIENDS AT RUBIE'S COSTUME COMPANY
THE LEADER IN LICENSED COSTUMES AND ACCESSORIES.
FOR MORE INFORMATION VISIT WWW.RUBIES.COM
MARVEL
© 2014 MARVEL

Mighty Avengers character designs.

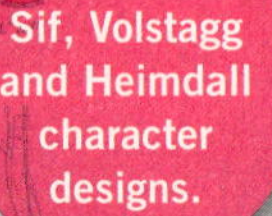

Sif, Volstagg and Heimdall character designs.

Avengers A.I. character designs.

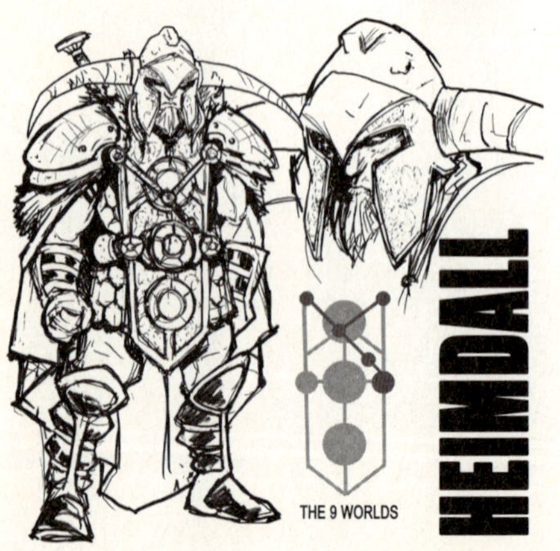

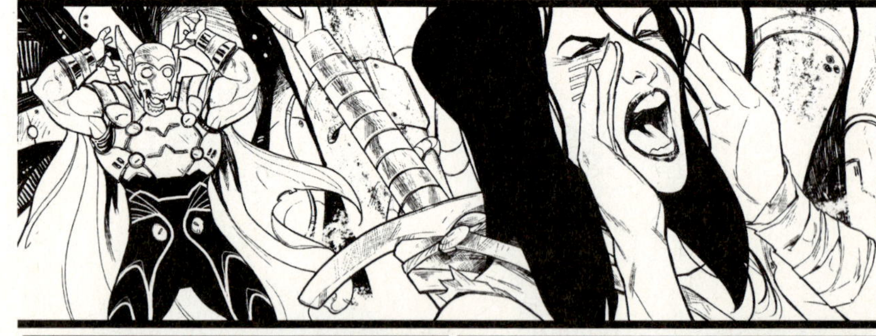

Sif and Beta Ray Bill from *Journey Into Mystery #655*, pencils and inks.

RYAN STEGMAN

FROM:
Grand Blanc, Michigan

FAVORITE CHARACTER TO DRAW:
Spider-Man

TITLE/CHARACTER YOU'D LOVE TO DRAW:
Thor

ARTISTIC INSPIRATION:
Katsuhiro Otomo, Todd McFarlane, Greg Capullo, Arthur Adams, Joe Madureira, Naoki Urasawa

FAVORITE ARTIST PEER:
Joe Madureira

CHECKLIST:
Amazing Spider-Man, Fantastic Four, Fear Itself: Hulk vs. Dracula, Incredible Hercules, Incredible Hulk, Magician: Apprentice, Marvel Adventures Spider-Man, Riftwar, Scarlet Spider, She-Hulks, Sif, Superior Spider-Man, X-23

Cover to *Superior Spider-Man #1*, pencils and inks.

Cover to *Wolverine (2014) #5*, pencils and inks.

Superior Spider-Man and Vulture from *Superior Spider-Man #3*, pencils and inks.

Wolverine and Beast from *Wolverine (2014) #4*, pencils.

TOYING AROUND WITH THE MARVEL LEGENDS

FISTS OF FURY: **Tired of getting sand kicked in your face? The Gamma Green Smash Fists can make a Hulk out of the puniest of weaklings.**

From the early days of the '60s to the bounty of today's offerings, the young and young-at-heart collectors of Marvel toys have never had it so good.

By Jess Harrold

MARVEL MEGOS:
Look out, Reed! Sue just can't take her eyes off Spidey's amazing set of wheels. (PHOTOS COURTESY OF BRIAN HEILER.)

KIDS THESE DAYS DON'T KNOW HOW LUCKY THEY ARE!

Recent products like Pottery Barn's Spider-Man bedding and Under Armour's Captain America workout gear mean today's True Believers-in-training can spend all day and night with their Marvel heroes. All-ages toys like Hasbro's *Super Hero Mashers*, a Spidey-themed *Operation* and LEGO versions of Cap, Thor — even Rocket Raccoon — can turn our children into lifelong Marvel zombies before they've even learned to read. Action-figure lines have run the gamut from Abomination to Zzzax—it happened in 1997's *Incredible Hulk Smash and Crash* line!—and provided endless entertainment for growing Marvelites…and their dads.

But it was not always thus. Past generations looking to "Make Mine Marvel" couldn't afford to be choosy—they had to take their favorite super heroes where they could find them. In fact, when eager web-heads finally got their hands on the very first Spider-Man doll in 1968, it wasn't even Peter Parker under the red-and-blues. It was some dude called Captain Action, an Ideal Toy Company figure whose range of costumes-sold-separately included those of Marvel heroes. "Captain Action was probably the most popular and best-remembered toy of the 1960s," Silver Age collector and enthusiast Lynch Lee Hymn recalls. "But I considered him a ripoff because he only dressed up as Spider-Man, Sgt. Fury and Captain America. He wasn't *actually* them."

But Captain Action did help get the ball rolling. The great Marvel merchandise machine really took off in the wake of the *Marvel Super Heroes* cartoon and the *Merry Marvel Marching Society* fan club. The industry giant of the time, Louis Marx & Co., produced friction and wind-up toys—but Hymn, who has made contributions to online and print guides to Silver Age Marvel toys, remembers these as "pretty much parodies of the characters" that didn't allow for imaginative adventures.

"The six hard plastic Marx figures of Spider-Man, Daredevil, Thor, Hulk, Iron Man and Captain America would be the first mass-produced action figures that became popular," Hymn says. "They were very detailed and extremely durable, but that was about it. They started off as gray or silver so you could paint them; later they were produced in solid, bright colors. They had no articulation, so many that are found today have stress marks on the arms where kids tried to bend them into poses. Also, they were great chew toys. It's rare to find any without bite marks. The favorite meals for kids were Daredevil's billy club, the thong on Thor's hammer and Spider-Man's fingers!"

Also very popular at the time were the *Easy Show* projector toys by Kenner, which brought Marvel heroes to life on your bedroom wall. "We wanted to see our super heroes, like on the newly televised *Marvel Super Heroes* cartoon," Hymn says. "And in a world without VHS or DVDs, this was closest to the real thing—unless you owned a 16mm projector. There were also the *Marvel Age Comic Spectacular* records that read the included comic to you word-for-word and with sound effects!"

GALACTIC LEGENDS:
The Guardians of the Galaxy... what a bunch of action figures!

But if you think the sky was the limit for Marvel toys during the 1960s, you'd be wrong. Heroes took to the air in two different lines of flying figures—with even the grounded types like Captain America, the Thing and Daredevil getting in on the action. These toys were pretty zany, Hymn remembers, even by Silver Age standards: "The *Marvel Flyers* by Topps were odd because the super heroes were in weird, awkward poses. The Ohio Arts *Flying Heroes* had a propeller on the top and bottom. It looked totally crazy back then, and still does today, but they did fly!"

Collector interest in these early Marvel items has also soared, with the Marx friction toys and a 1966 Captain America board game by Milton Bradley among the most sought-after. But there's no question what Hymn would put at the top of the Silver Age devotee's shopping list. "The Marvel Super Heroes Express Train by Marx is the Holy Grail," he says. "One sold for $8,800! The train is the grail because it was something that was not advertised on TV or in the comics back then. It was something that young Marvelites just stumbled upon at their local drugstore. Trains were favorites of kids back then, and to mix it with Marvel Comics characters was an added bonus. It also had a couple villains on it that were never shown on a Marvel toy again."

MARVEL MEETS MEGO

But as comic-book alchemy turned the Silver Age to Bronze, young fans still didn't have what they longed for: a line of poseable figures of their favorite heroes that would allow them to recreate the epic battles of their imaginations. In 1973, one of those children was in the right place to be heard, and a legendary Marvel toy line was born. "When Mego first launched their *World's Greatest Superheroes* line, it actually didn't have any Marvel characters," says Brian Heiler, curator of the online Mego Museum. "Rumor has it when Martin Abrams, president of Mego, showed his son the original line up, he asked, 'Where is Spider-Man?'

"The folks at Mego attribute their great success to being a young company that listened to children, and this was a good example. The rights for the Marvel characters were secured

IMPERATIVE ACTION:
Star-Lord, Gladiator, Blastaar, Medusa and Black Bolt hang out at San Diego Comic-Con in the Thanos Imperative exclusive set.

immediately. And even when the first four figures were released, the Marvel characters were already being shown on the packaging—even though they didn't actually hit the market until months later in the fall of 1973."

The Spider-Man Mego, which launched alongside Captain America, proved so popular that he was one of only three characters included in every super-hero toy line the company made, from 3.75" characters to bendy figures to talking stuffed dolls. But it is the 8" figures that have captured the imaginations of fans to this day.

MEGO ACTION FIGURES: **It's not easy being green—boxed-in Hulk and Green Goblin Megos just want to break free. (PHOTOS COURTESY OF BRIAN HEILER.)**

"While Ideal did a variation of the concept with their *Captain Action* costumes in the 1960s, Mego created the first true action figure of the hero itself," Heiler says. "It was no surprise kids went nuts for them. I think the combination of durable toys and bright, colorful packaging was just too perfect at the time. Add to it that daytime TV re-ran the *Spider-Man* cartoons and the *Incredible Hulk* TV series, and kids were crazy for super heroes."

The 13 Marvel 8" Mego dolls—which extended to the entire Fantastic Four, as well as surprising inclusions like the Falcon and the Lizard—cemented the line as the dominant Marvel toy of the era, ahead of rival products, Heiler says. "Mego really had the license sewn up in terms of action figures. The only other company matching their output was Azrak Hamway/Remco, who made a lot of lower-cost rack toys like Spider-Man helicopters and higher-priced stuff like inflatable Hulk muscles, which were kind of fun."

MARVEL SUPER HEROES EXPRESS TRAIN: **All aboard the ultra rare Marx toy! (PHOTO COURTESY OF LYNCH LEE HYMN.)**

One key appeal of the Megos was that Marvel fans could create "what if?" crossovers they'd never get to see in comics, because the company had tied up all the hot licenses of the day. "You could have Captain Kirk duke it out with the Green Goblin or have Spider-Man visit the Planet of the Apes," Heiler says. "That's definitely a big bonus to collectors today—the Mego lines embody the 1970s."

Far from stereotypical, nostalgic collectors decorating their homes with super-hero dolls defy classification. "I've met collectors from every walk of life," Heiler says, "from lawyers and doctors to Baptist ministers. Sometimes the only thing this group has in common is Mego."

SECRET WARS

While 1970s fans were able to invent their own merry Marvel Mego melees, one toy line a decade later provided the opportunity to recreate the epic battles of an actual comic book: the *Marvel Super Heroes Secret Wars* limited series. In 1984, Mattel brought major *Secret Wars* players like Dr. Doom and Cap into readers' homes in its toy line of the same name.

INFINITE GAUNTLET: **Hold reality in the palm of your hand, courtesy of this San Diego Comic-Con exclusive, with bonus *Infinite Series* figures!**

"(Marx figures)...were great chew toys. It's rare to find any without bite marks. The favorite meals for kids were Daredevil's billy club, the thong on Thor's hammer and Spider-Man's fingers!" – Collector Lynch Lee Hymn

MARX FIGURES: **Spidey puts his hands in the air like he don't care with this '60s-era toy. (PHOTOS COURTESY OF ALBERT BURR.)**

But when this Captain America threw his mighty shield, all those who chose to oppose him...had shields of their own! Fret not, though—all Cap's buddies packed defensive weaponry, too. And—get this—every "secret shield" carried a hidden message for comrades! That's something even Nick Fury never thought of. Such wackiness aside, the toys—though low on articulation by modern standards—captured the characters cleanly with unprecedented reverence to the comic-book page. But that's not surprising, given the line's origin.

"*Secret Wars* was really a comic limited series that was created for the toys," says Rob Rooney, editor-in-chief of *Raving Toy Maniac* magazine. "Mattel came up with the idea of doing a toy line supported by comics and pitched it to Jim Shooter, then-editor in chief of Marvel, and he ran with it.

"Besides Spider-Man's black costume, probably the thing most remembered from *Secret Wars* was the toy line. It really covered a nice selection of Marvel characters with heroes and villains. Iron Man is one of the standouts from the line, as was the Hobgoblin (who never appeared in the series)." Though the *Secret Wars* comic already featured a large cast, the toy line included other characters that didn't make it to Battleworld—such as Daredevil and Falcon. The entire third and final phase of releases, which only saw the light of day outside the United States, consisted entirely of *Secret Wars* absentees: Iceman, Electro and Constrictor. But that hasn't hurt the value of these rare figures, which remain highly sought-after by collectors.

"These figures are still popular today with a healthy secondary market, so clearly it was a hit with fans," Rooney says. "It definitely showed that a Marvel Comics-based toy line could succeed, and a few years later Toy Biz would start their own Marvel line that would eventually

MARVELMANIA CATALOGUE AD: **The Marvel Super Heroes have arrived! (COURTESY OF LYNCH LEE HYMN.)**

HAPPY RETURNS

Fantastic opportunity to really sit down and r
the entire series. I do hope that there are m
many more issues in the years to come!

Dear Merry Marvelites,

We were there, back when Banner used to turn grey; when Medusa first met Susan; when Sam partnered with Cap; when Murdock fell for Natchios. Our hearts leapt when Kitty faced the N'Garai, and smiled when Jessica married Luke. 75 years! Our company is nearly 125 now, but we still love our comics.

There is so much to be proud of, but we particularly want to say THANKS for your fantastic partnership. Our Diversity Council, teamed with MARVEL Custom, brought to life "Avengers: Heroes Welcome"; this book was featured in our five borough live seminar tour shared with over 500 New York Police Athletic League kids this summer. (They were REALLY terrific!)

Our Council members range from 25 to 80, speak 14 languages, and have backgrounds, hometowns, hobbies, passions, partners, skin tones and families as diverse as anyone could imagine. At our core, we absolutely know that people are not meant to be simply categorized. And we know that you believe this too; it's evident in every issue of every title you publish. MARVEL Comics reflect the full spectrum of the vibrancy that New York City represents, making certain that each of us, ALL of us, see ourselves reflected in your stories, and your heroes. Scratch that... OUR heroes.

So until Tony wears those roller skates again, we will MAKE OURS MARVEL.

Excelsior to all.

The BBDO Diversity Council
New York City

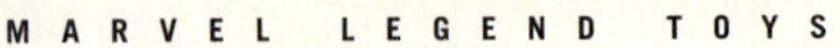

lead to today's explosion of Marvel action figures. Many of today's adults who are collecting Marvel action figures were the kids who first got hooked on them through *Secret Wars*."

SECRET WARS:
"Beyonder, your 11 o'clock is here." The Marvel Super Heroes (and villains) line up for their *Secret Wars*!

THE ERA OF LEGENDS BEGINS

That explosion of figures, fueled by lines based on Marvel's many successful cartoon series and movies in recent years, has unleashed a remarkable range of characters on an insatiable public—to the point where even devoted fans of Howard the Duck and Beta Ray Bill can display their heroes with pride. And no line has mined the Marvel canon like *Marvel Legends*. Launched by ToyBiz in 2002, then continued by Hasbro after they secured the license for Marvel toys in 2007, the *Legends* line has combined old-time classics like Fin Fang Foom with up-to-the-minute characters like the Superior Spider-Man—with plenty in-between immortalized in six inches of plastic.

Such diversity is part of the reason the *Legends* figures have proven to be enduringly popular in a competitive field, according to Hasbro Vice President of Global Brand Strategy & Marketing Adam Biehl. "The *Legends* line is great in so many ways, and we have to tip our hats to ToyBiz for creating a concept that's still just as relevant and sought-after today," he says.

One key feature Biehl cites is the Build-A-Figure bonus: *Legends* figures in a particular series each include one part of an additional, often large, character—further fueling the gotta-catch-'em-all frenzy for fans. "The BAF component has become such an essential and important piece of the *Legends* DNA," Biehl says. "We know that our fans love searching out their favorite figures, collecting all the pieces and assembling what is always an amazing figure!"

Another twist that's catnip for collectors is the hunt for "exclusive" figures released solely at the annual San Diego Comic-Con, often in boxed sets, which Biehl says have become some of the most desired pieces. Recent SDCC exclusives have included Ka-Zar, Shanna and Zabu, as well as a Thunderbolts pack. The 2014 Comic-Con boasted a *Thanos Imperative* collection featuring Black Bolt, Medusa, Gladiator and the comic-book version of a certain new movie star, Star-Lord. But for anyone holding out for their own miniature version of Chris Pratt as ol' Peter Quill, Hasbro has you covered.

MERC WITH A MASH-UP:
Something ain't quite right with Deadpool's healing factor in this Super Hero Masher.

As Biehl points out, "*Marvel Legends* is our opportunity to dive into 75 years of Marvel characters, costume styles, teams, stories and now movies! Marvel has become such a huge player in pop culture over the past several years. This has helped bring in an entirely new generation of Marvel fans that may not have grown up reading comic books but now have the same access through all these great films, and the same affinity for these characters. This has allowed us to create a broader toy range and have tons of fun playing with the Marvel Universe."

INFINITE POSSIBILITIES

The widespread success of the Marvel Cinematic Universe and other movies based on Marvel characters has led to a rebranding of the line as the *Marvel Legends Infinite Series*, with a shift in focus to themed character sets tying in with each year's hot films—including summer 2014's *Guardians of the Galaxy* (with Groot as the Build-A-Figure bonus!). Biehl describes the change as a strategic decision to concentrate merchandise within the individual franchise properties. "By taking this approach, our goal was to not only continue to appeal to our core collectors, but also reach a new generation of fans and kids alike," he says. "This also allowed us to create a stronger presence at retail with more characters. Our strategy is proving to be successful, as we've seen tremendous sell-through." But fear not, comic-book traditionalists: Hasbro isn't turning its back on the stars of the printed page! Thematically relevant comic versions are still included, such as Nova and Cosmic Iron Man in the "Groot series." As Biehl puts it, "We try to make them all!"

The *Infinite Series* branding has also been applied to Hasbro's 3.75" figures, formerly known as the *Marvel Universe* line—as has a sprinkle of SDCC magic. This year's truly cosmic exclusive is an *Infinity Gauntlet* set that includes a wearable version of the all-powerful glove. The choice between the larger *Marvel Legends Infinite Series* and the smaller *Infinite Series* is all about personal preference for fans, according to Biehl. "Some fans collect by character and some collect by scale, so we have two fantastic lines that allow collectors and kids to express their fandom for Marvel any way they choose," he says.

Speaking of kids, Hasbro has offered plenty of opportunities for parents to introduce their children to Marvel at an early age—from the hyper-successful *Super Hero Squad* line of stylized collectible characters that spawned a cartoon and a comic book to the current body-swapping glory of the *Super Hero Mashers*. "With the *Super Hero Mashers*, we know that children love the power to create and customize," Biehl says. "*Super Hero Mashers* allows them to mix and mash their favorite super heroes to create the ultimate—and funniest!—super hero they can ever imagine! What kid doesn't want to give Spider-Man the smashing power of Hulk or the repulsor-blasting action of Iron Man? These toys work because it puts the power of storytelling into their hands."

Putting things into—and onto—kids' hands has reaped major dividends in Hasbro's wider toy range, too. As Biehl reminds, "Everyone loves a good set of Hulk Fists!" Those gamma-green, smash-hit mitts—as well as fun versions of Cap's shield, Iron Man's helmet and gauntlets, Thor's hammer, Hawkeye's bow, and Spidey's web-shooters—enable children across the world to play as their idols.

"As more kids become super-hero fans, our role-play toys for Iron Man, Hulk, Thor, Captain America and Spider-Man have become some of our top sellers," Biehl says. "These toys allow kids to recreate

MARVEL FLYERS: **Is it a bird? Is it a plane? No, it's...Daredevil? Flyers (left) and box art (below). (PHOTOS COURTESY OF LYNCH LEE HYMN.)**

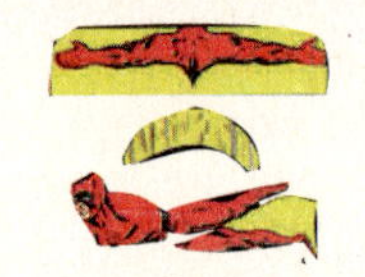

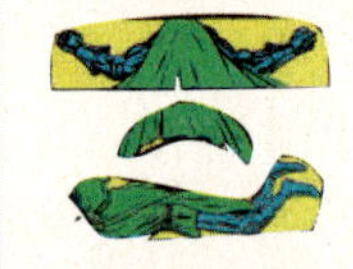

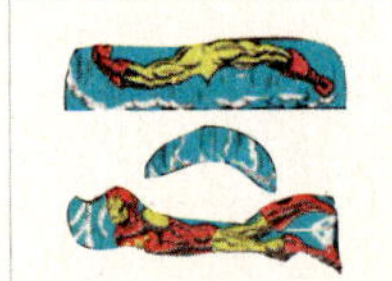

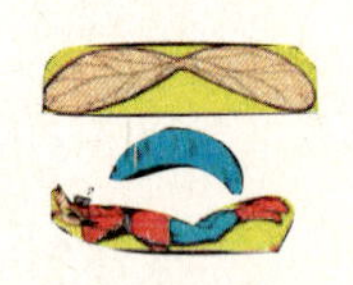
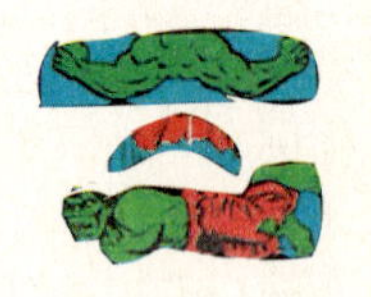

their favorite super-hero moments from the movies and animated shows. At Hasbro, we are proud to offer the widest and deepest selection of Marvel toys in the world. Whether you are young or old, like action figures or games, or just want to dress up your Mr. Potato Head like Spider-Man, we have the Marvel toy for you!"

And as Marvel heads into its next 75 years, there's no sign of letting up. Biehl is sure of it: "The future is bright! We're excited to continue to bring the Marvel Universe to life with our action figures to kids and collectors alike. We are super excited about Marvel's *Avengers: Age of Ultron*, as well as all the amazing Marvel Studios animated shows. Of course, we will continue to excite fans with expansion of our *Infinite Series* product lines—with more new figure reveals to come soon!"

There's just no fighting it. This is the mighty Marvel age of toys! •

CLOAK AND DAGGER
NO MERE WORDS OF OURS CAN TRULY DESCRIBE THE TENDERNESS OF THIS MOMENT... SO WE WONT EVEN TRY!
She-HULK

DOWNLOAD THE REVOLUTION

Axel Alonso, Jim Nausedas, and Ron Perazza talk Marvel's Digital Revolution

By Tim Stevens

To say Marvel Comics has been in the digital comics game as long as the Internet has existed turns out to be nearly accurate. Embracing the possibility of online comics with Marvel CyberComics in 1996 — a full year before the International Telecommunications Union even began to study what percent of the population was accessing the Internet — the House of Ideas beat everyone to the punch. Less than 11 percent of the developed world used the web, but Marvel had content ready for even those limited few.

"Marvel took a very progressive approach to digital comics, investing both time and resources to discovering how technology could affect graphic storytelling," Consultant to Marvel on Digital Publishing Ron Perazza remembers. "In the '90s, that was through experimentation with integrating animation, sound and even voiceover with things like Marvel's CyberComics and the Excelsior Theater."

Eighteen years later, Internet usage has risen to an estimated 78 percent, and Marvel has redefined its approach to digital comics to better serve that exploding population. Today, with more than 15,000 comics in its database, the Marvel Unlimited subscription service is a massive storehouse of Marvel's four-color history that allows fans to access Engleheart's *Avengers #118* and Hickman's *New Avengers #13* with equal ease. Additionally, the Marvel Comics App, Marvel AR content, Infinite Comics and the free digital codes available on many of Marvel's physical comics demonstrate the company's dedication to the digital platform.

"Marvel's approach to digital comics has really evolved lock-step with how the digital marketplace has changed, and I think we've done a great job at staying at the crest of that wave," Sales Director Jim Nausedas says.

Evidence of this evolution is seen in Marvel's insistence on updating Marvel Unlimited to keep pace with technology.

"When Marvel Unlimited launched in 2007, it was a streaming desktop subscription service that was really the only outlet for digital comics," Nausedas recalls. "At that time, mobile devices hadn't yet exploded, and it wasn't until 2010 that the Marvel Comics App launched, offering single issues for purchase. Since then, the Marvel Comics App and Marvel Unlimited service have continued to grow and evolve, both offering a great comics reading experience."

"The formats and devices may have changed, but Marvel's approach has been remarkably constant," Perazza echoes. "Marvel lives up to the 'House of Ideas' moniker not just through the content it produces, but also in its approach. They love pushing the envelope and exploring how technology could be used to advance digital storytelling, and recent efforts like Infinite Comics, Marvel's AR program and Adaptive Audio are testament to that spirit of innovation."

While some worry that the rise in digital's ubiquity as both an avenue of creative production and a place to access comics may signal an end to the physical production of comics, Editor in Chief Axel Alonso sees no reason for concern.

"The digital platform is extremely important to the evolution of our business and, in fact, the way we tell comic-book stories," he explains. "That said, we view digital and print as being complementary. Digital distribution provides a newsstand to attract new readers, who might very well become the next wave of foot traffic at comic-book stores and other places our readers find print comics."

"These digital innovations are great for new or casual readers," Nausedas agrees. "I think the very offering of a digital comic itself is huge for people who may love Marvel characters and are looking to read their first comic, or for a person looking to get back into reading comics. Offering comics anytime and anywhere has opened up a giant new pool of potential Marvel readers across the world."

Alonso also points out that the digital format can be a boon to titles that might have otherwise slipped through the cracks.

"It's all been positive," he says. "It's a thrill to see newer titles, like the recent *Ms. Marvel* comic, explode as digital purchases."

Of course, the Marvel Comics App and Marvel Unlimited hardly represent the only ways the House of Ideas has sought to increase fan access. The Marvel AR app, Infinite Comics and Adaptive Audio have all sprung from the digital platform to change the ways readers can enjoy comics and interact with their favorite characters, writers and artists.

Unsurprisingly, even those at Marvel have their favorite digital offerings. For instance, both Alonso and Nausedas have tremendous affection for Infinite Comics.

"These are comics that use the unique tools of the handheld device to tell stories," Alonso says. "Writer and artist use the widescreen format to tell a story that is unique. The reader swipes the screen to see new images unfold. The familiar tropes of comics — panels, balloons, captions — are still there, but the reader still controls the pace of the read. We've done a few, and we learn something new with each new exploration of the medium. And as the technology improves, we take advantage of that."

"I'd have to say I'm very partial to Infinite Comics," Nausedas affirms. "With each new Infinite Comic, the creators have really explored the limits as to what new possibilities comics can reach in the digital space. The *Deadpool: The Gauntlet* series was fantastic, and the *Wolverine* and *Iron Man* series both impressed me. They come across as the next evolutionary step in comics, without straying away from what makes comics enjoyable in the first place."

Nausedas also professes his enjoyment of behind-the-scenes content.

"I'm always a fan of seeing behind the curtain," he says. "Reading the script, and then reading the finished comic to see how the artist and writer work together to create a comic is incredible. We've begun offering a few digital Special Editions for some select titles, like *Amazing Spider-Man #1* and the *Original Sin* series, that showcase some of these behind-the-scenes extras. I'd love to build on that and make that content more integrated with digital comics as a whole."

Perazza holds up Adaptive Audio as his favorite advancement of the digital revolution.

"When I rejoined Marvel in early 2013, Dan Buckley challenged me with trying to figure out how to integrate audio in a digital comic in a way that enhanced the reading experience but still allowed the reader to control it and in fact responded to how they read," he says. "He had a vision of what it could be and tasked me with figuring out how to make it happen — and how to make it happen so that the final result was still a comic book that preserved the essential qualities of graphic storytelling. It was definitely a challenge not just from a technological or editorial point of view, but even just trying to get everyone to wrap their heads around what it was! In the end, though, we had a great team and excellent development partners who were all focused on producing a quality experience. I'm extremely proud of that project."

To provide readers with the best in digital offerings, Marvel must always look forward while enjoying its current success. The members of the Marvel team remain aware of the evolving technology, as well as the possible challenges on the horizon — and they're confident that those challenges represent opportunities to provide even stronger online content.

"We're keeping up with the technology, not being afraid to take chances or cut losses," Alonso says. "Making sure that our retail partners are always aware that we consider them just that: partners. We are in this together."

Nausedas sees the digital platforms as chances for the readers to connect not only with individual comics, but also to become enamored with the Marvel Universe as a whole.

"One area I look to as both a challenge and an opportunity is finding a way to guide new readers into easy entry points in the digital space, and helping current readers understand how different comic stories interweave and connect with each other," he says. "One of the greatest things about the Marvel Universe is how all of the comics feel connected, and repercussions in one title can be felt across several others.

"We've got some great stuff in the pipeline that is going to help create a roadmap or a guide for people through the Marvel Universe. There are so many great Marvel stories, and I think it's part of our job to showcase these stories for all."

Perazza notes that the challenges and opportunities of the future are aligned with encouraging and then meeting an increasing readership.

"The great challenge for digital comics is the same today as it was years ago: growth," he says. "The last few years have shown amazing, steady adoption of digital comics as more and more readers discover Marvel's apps and content. And yet it's still a relatively new area, poised for massive growth. The challenge is organizing decades of content and providing it in a logical, easy-to-access way. The opportunity there is to be able to reach a truly vast, worldwide audience of fans."

While no one can say exactly what comes next, what stands clear is Marvel's commitment to giving readers the most intuitive and fulfilling reading experience possible.

"We've got some great stuff in the pipeline that is going to amaze," Nausedas concludes. "It's an exciting time to be reading digital comics." •

MARVEL STUDIOS

BUILDING A NEW UNIVERSE

BY JESS HARROLD WITH JOHN RHETT THOMAS

As 2006 dawned, almost seven decades of comics, cartoons, toys and more had firmly established Marvel's heroes among the pantheon of pop-culture icons. But back then, if you picked a non-comics reader at random, from anywhere across the world, and asked them who their favorite Marvel super hero was, 9 out of 10 likely would have said Spider-Man, Wolverine or maybe the Hulk. The success of licensed movies starring Spidey and the X-Men, and the historic affection for the *Incredible Hulk* TV show, amply demonstrates how the big — and small — screen can entrench a literary figure in the public consciousness.

Now, only eight years later, the average person may find it difficult to pick a favorite. Captain America is a worldwide icon. Thor is riding high, more popular than he's been for centuries. Hulk is a smash hit once again, with a legion of new fans. Ask a passerby in Japan right this minute, and they might mention a certain talking raccoon. A Russian film fanatic may be partial to the Winter Soldier. Next year, a moviegoer in France could well exclaim "L'Ant-Man!" And Iron Man? He has a good case for being the most popular character in movies, full stop. In five years, there's no telling who might top your own list.

And it's all thanks to Marvel's decision, after years of licensing characters from Blade to the Fantastic Four with varying success, to enter the movie business for real. With Kevin Feige installed as president, the new Marvel Studios built a plan for box-office domination, investing half a billion dollars to launch an initial pair of blockbusters, released a month apart. Half a billion dollars is high stakes, and a losing bet could have crippled Marvel's ambitions — not just at theaters, but companywide. Thankfully, Marvel's numbers came up — in a big way.

As we celebrate Marvel's 75th birthday, perhaps nothing will shape the next 75 years more than its continuing silver-screen success. Join us on a trip back through the last eight years, and ten movies, to see how this Marvel Cinematic Universe took shape — from the casting triumphs to the bold storytelling choices — with a special focus on the one ingredient that binds it all together. No, not Phil Coulson. Awesome visual effects.

IRON MAN

May 2, 2008

WORLDWIDE GROSS: $585 million (#99 all time as of July 2014, figures courtesy of Box Office Mojo)
CHARACTERS INTRODUCED: Iron Man/Tony Stark, Pepper Potts, Obadiah Stane, Jim Rhodes, Agent Phil Coulson, Nick Fury, Happy Hogan, Jarvis
DIRECTOR: Jon Favreau
SCREENPLAY BY: Mark Fergus & Hawk Ostby and Art Marcum & Matt Holloway
OSCAR NOMINATIONS: Best Visual Effects, Best Sound Editing

THE PRODUCERS SIMPLY wanted to launch a franchise. They wound up launching a whole darn universe. Robert Downey Jr. — always a critically acclaimed actor — became a mega-star with the role of Tony Stark, a part he seems born to play. Gwyneth Paltrow and Jeff Bridges signed on for the roles of "Girl Friday" Pepper Potts and adversary Obadiah Stane, adding to the star caliber of Marvel's first feature film. But arguably the biggest coup was the crew of special-effects masters, including armor designer Stan Winston, who helped bring the high-tech world of Iron Man to cutting-edge, 21st-century life. With Marvel artist Adi Granov — who had already revolutionized the way Shellhead was drawn in his series of covers and his *Extremis* collaboration with writer Warren Ellis — on board as a consultant, filmmakers delivered a Golden Avenger ripped from the modern comic-book page. But there's no doubt that the biggest thrill for fans came right at the very end. In a brief scene that taught audiences to always, always stick around for the whole credits of a Marvel film, Samuel L. Jackson donned the famous eyepatch as a Nick Fury who looked like he just stepped out of a Bryan Hitch page from *The Ultimates*. His invitation to Stark to join the "Avengers Initiative" pointed firmly to the future and offered a sign that no matter how huge fans thought *Iron Man* was going to be, Marvel had even bigger plans ahead.

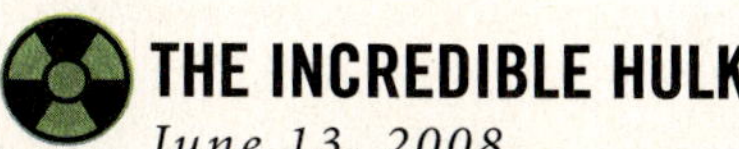

THE INCREDIBLE HULK

June 13, 2008

WORLDWIDE GROSS: $263 million (#392 all time)
CHARACTERS INTRODUCED: Hulk/Bruce Banner, Betty Ross, General Thunderbolt Ross, The Abomination/Emil Blonsky, Samuel Sterns, Leonard Samson
DIRECTOR: Louis Leterrier
SCREEN STORY AND SCREENPLAY BY: Zak Penn

IRON MAN WAS still riding high at cinemas when *The Incredible Hulk* bowed in the summer of 2008. While not the box-office sensation that its predecessor was, it managed to perform a crucial task for Marvel's Phase One plans: It restored the Hulk to prominence after the 2003 Ang Lee-directed *Hulk* proved to be a noble misfire, and set the stage for the character's inclusion in *Marvel's The Avengers*. With Edward Norton portraying Bruce Banner, *The Incredible Hulk* returned the "on the run" motif from the classic TV series to prominence — with director Louis Leterrier also inspired by Bruce Jones' similarly themed comic-book arc, and Jeph Loeb and Tim Sale's classic *Hulk: Gray*. According to Leterrier, the whole subject of the movie is an "anti-arc" in which Banner begins to accept his alter ego. "We start with the Hulk and Banner being real opposites, although they inhabit kind of the same exterior," he said. "But it's really the Jekyll and Hyde — a very obvious theme. And the whole journey of Bruce Banner is to understand that monster within, that monster which eventually becomes the hero within." Leterrier worked closely with star Edward Norton and recalled a comment from the actor about his character: "The anti-hero, the oppressed man...if you mess with him you will get the righteous bite-back. That's what people love. It's justice after all. The grander justice that comes through super-powers."

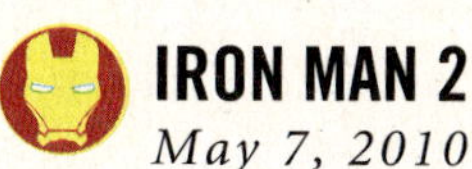

IRON MAN 2

May 7, 2010

WORLDWIDE GROSS: $624 million (#84 all-time)
DIRECTOR: Jon Favreau
SCREENPLAY BY: Justin Theroux
OSCAR NOMINATION: Best Visual Effects
CHARACTERS INTRODUCED: War Machine, Black Widow/Natasha Romanoff, Justin Hammer, Whiplash/Ivan Vanko, Howard Stark

IRON MAN 2 explores the ramifications of Tony Stark's fateful proclamation to the world at the end of his first movie: "I am Iron Man." As Feige put it: "He's been Iron Man for six months...If he was the most famous man in America in the first movie, he's the most famous man in the world in this movie." In that rapid rise to global fame, life imitates art. "It's hard to believe now, but two years ago, not everybody knew Iron Man," Feige said at the time. "It was a phenomenon of the year, and for us at Marvel — everybody knows Iron Man now." Tony is now a war profiteer turned peacemaker — but starved of Stark weaponry, the military wants to get its hands on the Iron Man armor. With Tony's health beginning to fail, rival industrialist Justin Hammer makes a play for the government dollar. The sequel fittingly expands the Iron Man mythos with armored innovations, including a suitcase suit inspired by the Silver Age comics and the augmented War Machine model piloted by James Rhodes. But perhaps most significantly, another spot of perfect casting sees Scarlett Johansson join the Marvel team as Natasha Romanoff, spying on Stark Enterprises for S.H.I.E.L.D. Grabbing the limelight in one of the film's best action sequences, Johansson whets the appetite for more Black Widow in the future.

THOR

May 6, 2011

WORLDWIDE GROSS: $449 million (#157 all time)
DIRECTOR: Kenneth Branagh
STORY BY: J. Michael Straczynski and Mark Protosevich
SCREENPLAY BY: Ashley Edward Miller & Zack Stentz and Don Payne
CHARACTERS INTRODUCED: Thor, Loki, Odin, Heimdall, Sif, Fandral, Hogun, Volstagg, Frigga, Jane Foster, Erik Selvig, Darcy Lewis, Jasper Sitwell, Hawkeye

"THOR IS one of our more challenging characters," Co-Producer Craig Kyle said. "He's the least Marvel-ish of them — he's a god, he's an alien. So the way we tried to tackle that challenge was to translate that story in a way that would make Thor fans happy, but would also get people like my wife to enjoy the story." Sweetening the deal, Chris Hemsworth proved himself well worthy to wield the hammer of Thor. But to many, Tom Hiddleston as the Thunder God's trickster half-brother stole the movie, perhaps aptly. "The first *Thor* movie was as much a Loki origin story as it was a Thor origin story," Feige acknowledged. "I really wanted the Marvel Cinematic Universe to have a villain as interesting as Magneto was in the first X-Men film." Loki would go on to fully realize that potential in *Marvel's The Avengers*. Meanwhile, *Thor's* director Kenneth Branagh brought the gravitas of his extensive Shakespearean experience, working with concept artist Charlie Wen to bring Asgard and its denizens to life. "Drawing inspiration from the Jack Kirby comics, we forged ahead into crafting an interesting and otherworldly set of personalities," Wen said. The recipe proved a success.

CAPTAIN AMERICA: THE FIRST AVENGER

July 22, 2011

WORLDWIDE GROSS: $371 million (#217 all time)
DIRECTOR: Joe Johnston
SCREENPLAY BY: Christopher Markus & Stephen McFeely
CHARACTERS INTRODUCED: Captain America/Steve Rogers, "Bucky" Barnes, the Howling Commandos, Peggy Carter, Red Skull, Arnim Zola, Hydra

CASTING CHRIS EVANS as Captain America raised eyebrows, as the actor had earlier flamed on as the Human Torch in two *Fantastic Four* films — and blond hair apart, Steve Rogers and Johnny Storm are not known for their similarities. But Evans proved he had the versatility to play a very different hero. "If you look at our other films, you see that we cast performers first," *Captain America* Co-Producer Stephen Broussard said. "We make sure that we cast actors with real talent, with real acting chops, and that's certainly going to be the case with a character like Steve Rogers. He's a very complex character. He starts in one place and ends up in a completely different place, both physically and emotionally. You need someone who can play the broad range of that. You also need someone who, when we get to *Marvel's The Avengers*, can go toe-to-toe with actors like Robert Downey Jr. — someone who can hold their own in a scene." Speaking of physical transformations, the movie's stand-out SFX work features Evans' face somehow inhabiting the body of skinny weakling Steve Rogers when the film begins during World War II. While the bulk of the action takes place during the war, with Cap and his allies fighting the Red Skull and the forces of Hydra, the very end sees Cap revived in the modern day after years on ice. And as the film's subtitle suggests, the stage is set for...

MARVEL'S THE AVENGERS

May 4, 2012

WORLDWIDE GROSS: $1.519 billion (#3 all time)
DIRECTOR: Joss Whedon
STORY BY: Zak Penn and Joss Whedon
SCREENPLAY BY: Joss Whedon
OSCAR NOMINATION: Best Visual Effects
CHARACTERS INTRODUCED: Agent Maria Hill, the Chitauri, Thanos, World Security Council

KEY TO MARVEL Studios' success so far had been the marriage of inspired casting with directors who had something to say. With *Marvel's The Avengers* (the title demonstrating how the Marvel name had come to be a powerful brand in itself), pretty much all the stars were already aligned. What was needed was a man in the chair with the ability to assemble Earth's Mightiest Heroes in a single movie. And the guy who took the megaphone was perhaps Marvel's boldest choice yet. Joss Whedon came with the TV pedigree of shows like *Buffy the Vampire Slayer*, *Angel* and *Firefly* — not to mention a big following in the comic-book community. But his big-screen resume offered little evidence he could deliver a billion-dollar summer tentpole movie. Good thing Marvel Studios is prepared to think outside the box. As Feige put it: "We needed somebody who could take a big story and a big idea, and execute it without ever letting the characters get lost amongst all the spectacle." Having proved himself the master of ensemble TV, Whedon did exactly that with the Avengers. Cap, Thor, Iron Man, Black Widow and Hawkeye all get their share of big moments, both action-packed and comedic.

Tom Hiddleston, continuing his charismatic portrayal as Loki, almost succeeds in making the villain more popular than the heroes. But there's no doubt about the movie's breakout star: Whedon delivers a cinematic Hulk exactly as fans had imagined him. Two standout scenes had audiences worldwide cheering and laughing in equal measure, and in Mark Ruffalo — the big screen's third Bruce Banner — Marvel finally had a keeper. "The release of *Marvel's The Avengers* is the realization of a dream that began long before I was born — when Stan Lee, Jack Kirby and everyone in the Marvel Bullpen had the brilliant idea to put all these characters together in one comic book to deal with one big mega-event," Producer Jeremy Latcham said. "When we became our own studio, our endgame was to one day combine them all." With a box-office bounty beaten only by cinematic phenomena *Titanic* and *Avatar*, *Marvel's The Avengers* not only delivered what fans wanted — it went beyond their wildest dreams.

IRON MAN 3

May 3, 2013

WORLDWIDE GROSS: $1.215 billion (#6 all time)
DIRECTOR: Shane Black
SCREENPLAY BY: Drew Pearce & Shane Black
OSCAR NOMINATION: Best Visual Effects
CHARACTERS INTRODUCED: Aldrich Killian, Maya Hansen, Mandarin, Iron Patriot

FOR *IRON MAN 3*, Favreau may have stepped out of the director's chair, but he remained very much part of the team by reprising his role as Happy Hogan. Taking Favreau's place behind the camera, Shane Black delivered a tale that focused on a Tony Stark whose world has been rocked by the events of *Marvel's The Avengers*. "*Iron Man 3* is very much inspired by the first half of *Iron Man*," Feige said. "We've always said, let's get Tony back to the cave, where he's backed up against a wall and he's got to use his intelligence to get out of it. He can't call Thor, he can't call Cap, he can't call Nick Fury, and he can't look for the Helicarrier in the sky." Ushering in the second phase of the Marvel Cinematic Universe, *Iron Man 3* demonstrated that the studio was not interested in the easy option of giving the public more of the same. From the personal angst suffered by Stark to the bold take on Iron Man's arch-foe the Mandarin — albeit one that would polarize ardent comic-book fans — this was a film that explored fresh territory, both for the character and in terms of the conventional structure of a super-hero film. Though the visual language of the *Iron Man* films was well-established, one of the third's main innovations is the legion of artificially intelligent armors Tony can call on in his hour of need. "We built 41 suits for this movie," Executive Producer and EVP of VFX and Post-Production Victoria Alonso said. "One of our biggest, most complicated challenges was that every suit had to have a personality and a look that audiences could enjoy. We've never seen multiples of these suits before, and now we have a phenomenal 22-minute sequence that completely rocks. We're able to display all the artificial intelligence that Tony Stark created, in a pretty phenomenal way."

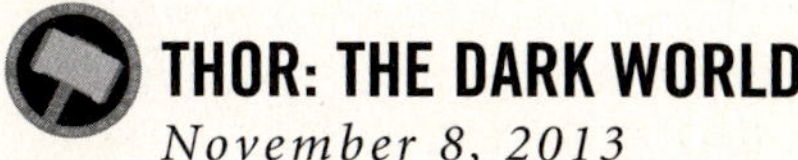

THOR: THE DARK WORLD

November 8, 2013

WORLDWIDE GROSS: $645 million (#78 all time)
DIRECTOR: Alan Taylor
STORY BY: Don Payne and Robert Rodat
SCREENPLAY BY: Christopher L. Yost and Christopher Markus & Stephen McFeely
CHARACTERS INTRODUCED: Malekith, Kurse, Tyr, The Collector

THE THEME OF progression in Phase Two of the Marvel Cinematic Universe is evident in *Thor: The Dark World*, in which the Thunder God faces the villainous elf Malekith in a story drawn from Walter Simonson's seminal run on the *Thor* title. "Thor is not the petulant son that he was in the first film," Executive Producer Craig Kyle said. "Not to say he's not still flawed. He absolutely is. He's just not that same man who was all heart and no mind. He's finding more center to his character." Meanwhile, the world Thor inhabits has also evolved under the watchful eye of new director Alan Taylor, whose talent for grounding fantasy with an air of reality is evident on TV phenomenon *Game of Thrones*. Kevin Feige praised Taylor's visual approach to the film: "Alan is bringing a grittier, more visceral, more textured patina to the designs of the worlds — and to Asgard, in particular. It's less to chase either *Game of Thrones* or *Lord of the Rings*, because you're not going to catch up. But part of the fun of Thor, over our other characters, is he doesn't have to stay on Earth." The harsher aesthetic reflects the terrible threat Thor must face during a film in which the stakes are raised and the consequences will be lasting. *The Dark World* offers a platform for Loki to shine once more, while a visually stunning climactic battle provides tantalizing glimpses of more of the Nine Realms.

CAPTAIN AMERICA: THE WINTER SOLDIER

April 4, 2014

WORLDWIDE GROSS: $713 million (#62 all time)
DIRECTORS: Anthony & Joe Russo
SCREENPLAY BY: Christopher Markus & Stephen McFeely
CHARACTERS INTRODUCED: Winter Soldier, Alexander Pierce, Falcon/Sam Wilson, Brock Rumlow, Agent 13

ACADEMY AWARD-WINNER Robert Redford in a comic-book movie? Believe it. Of course, it's a lot more plausible when the comic-book movie in question has the tone of a taut '70s spy thriller. Though most known for their comedic work, brothers and directors Anthony and Joe Russo took the *Cap* sequel in a whole different direction, drawing inspiration from the films of William Friedkin and Brian De Palma — most notably *The French Connection* and *Blow Out*. "We tried to give the characters clear aims, most often survival or escape," the brothers explained. "And then attempted to complicate those aims through narrative. Nick Fury's hubris makes him vulnerable. Steve Rogers' disenfranchisement keeps him off balance. We then tried to follow Friedkin and De Palma's example by creating long sequences filled with mini-narratives where the characters' aims are constantly in danger of being thwarted." The plot sees Cap still finding his place in the modern world, only to be confronted by a ghost from his past in the form of the Winter Soldier — just nine years after the character was introduced in writer Ed Brubaker's run on the *Captain America* comic. The mature and suspenseful plot leads to a major upheaval in the status quo of the Marvel Cinematic Universe — one that had immediate game-changing consequences for the TV spinoff *Marvel's Agents of S.H.I.E.L.D.*, as Marvel's continuing drive to push boundaries saw the interwoven continuity of its cinematic output now even cross media. The Russos were quick to praise Visual Effects Supervisor Dan DeLeeuw for his "intelligence, artistry, tenacity and encyclopedic knowledge," which helped sculpt the film's 2,400 special-effects shots into works of art.

GUARDIANS OF THE GALAXY

August 1, 2014

DIRECTOR: James Gunn

WRITTEN BY: James Gunn and Nicole Perlman

CHARACTERS INTRODUCED: Star-Lord/Peter Quill, Gamora, Rocket, Groot, Drax, Nebula, Ronan, Yondu, Rhomann Dey, Nova Prime Irani Rael

IF THERE IS one word that sums up Marvel Studios in 2014, it's "confidence." With the second phase of the MCU nearing its culmination, films like *Iron Man 3* and *Captain America: The Winter Soldier* shocked fans and challenged cinemagoers' expectations of what constitutes a super-hero movie. By selecting *Guardians of the Galaxy* as their tenth motion picture, Marvel Studios proves its determination to defy predictions is stronger than ever. Sure, they have succeeded in making household names of Iron Man, Cap and Thor, but these characters each have at least 50 years of publishing history behind them. The Guardians of the Galaxy count just over 100 issues, while the movie lineup — drawn from Dan Abnett and Andy Lanning's 2008 reinvention of the team — featured characters largely forgotten or unknown. "I think *Guardians of the Galaxy* is the boldest film we've made since the first *Iron Man* in terms of it being unexpected," Feige said. But as Executive Producer and EVP of VFX and Post-Production Victoria Alonso points out, once you set the bar with *Avengers*, where do you go from there? "You don't go higher," she said. "You take a left turn and you do *Guardians of the Galaxy*." But when producers first told eventual director James Gunn about the project, he wasn't convinced. "It was pretty apparent to me Marvel had lost their minds," he said, pointing in particular to how audiences would react to a gun-toting raccoon. But as he drove home, resolved to say no, he was hit by a lightning bolt realization: "*Guardians of the Galaxy* was the movie I had been waiting my whole life to do." Seizing the chance to help create a space opera for a 21st-century audience, he set about making a movie with a very different visual than most modern science fiction, so often beholden to the dark look of classics like *Alien* and *Blade Runner*. "*Guardians of the Galaxy* would be about color, and life," he said. "In-your-face, over-the-top COLOR. We would rescue the aesthetics of pulpy science-fiction films from the '50s and '60s while simultaneously retaining the grittiness and workaday reality of later films. And the raccoon, the raccoon that initially seemed to be such a hurdle — the raccoon was the best part. We would completely deconstruct and build back up the anthropomorphic animal." And all that with a '70s soundtrack. Gunn was full of praise for the talented array of concept artists and SFX teams that gave life to his vision, claiming that their depictions of Rocket and Groot "regularly move me to tears." The bravado, the swagger, that made *Guardians of the Galaxy* possible was never more in evidence than in its first hilarious trailer, set to the strains of Blue Swede's "Hooked on a Feeling." As Star-Lord, Rocket and the rest of the A-holes Ooga-Chaka-ed their way to the attention of an unprepared public, buzz quickly built for a movie that promised to be unlike anything audiences had seen before. You will believe a raccoon can fly.

*And the wild ride is only just beginning, with a multitude of major Marvel motion pictures in our future. From the cosmic (*Guardians of the Galaxy*) we head to the microscopic (*Ant-Man*, 2015); from A.I. sci-fi (*Avengers: Age of Ultron*, 2015) we could segue to the supernatural (*Doctor Strange*, watch this space!). There's absolutely no telling where this journey will end. Or which of the Marvel Universe's uncanny locations we'll visit along the way!* •

10¢
MARVEL COMICS
OCT.
This Month
"THE HUMAN TORCH"
"THE ANGEL"
"SUBMARINER"
"MASKED RAIDER"
Featuring
KA-ZAR THE GREAT
12 PAGES OF JUNGLE ADVENTURE!
ACTION
MYSTERY
ADVENTURE